Evolving PLaneT

Four Billion Years of Life on Earth

ERICA KELLY & RICHARD KISSEL

Published in association with The Field Museum, Chicago

ABRAMS BOOKS FOR YOUNG READERS, NEW YORK

For Gretchen
—E.K. & R.K.

The exhibition *Evolving Planet* is made possible by Kenneth and Anne Griffin.

Elizabeth Morse Genius Charitable Trust is the generous sponsor of *Evolving Planet*'s Genius Hall of Dinosaurs.
Evolving Planet received support from the Illinois Department of Commerce and Economic Opportunity, the U.S. Department of
Housing and Urban Development, the U.S. Department of Energy, and the U.S. Department of Education.

We are most appreciative of the many generous donors supporting *Evolving Planet*.

Library of Congress Cataloging-in-Publication Data

Kelly, Erica.
Evolving planet / by Erica Kelly and Richard Kissel.
p. cm.
1. Earth—Exhibitions. 2. Field Museum of Natural History—Exhibitions. I. Kissel, Richard A., 1975– II. Title.
QE501.K385 2008
551—dc22
2007036342

Book design by Maria T. Middleton

Printed and bound in China
10 9 8 7 6 5 4 3 2 1

HNA ▉▉▉▉▉
harry n. abrams, inc.
a subsidiary of La Martinière Groupe

115 West 18th Street
New York, NY 10011
www.hnabooks.com

Contents

Acknowledgments

The Field Museum is grateful to Kenneth and Anne Griffin, whose support made *Evolving Planet* possible. The exhibition is named in their honor.

Our thanks go to Elizabeth Morse Genius Charitable Trust, the sponsor of *Evolving Planet*'s Hall of Dinosaurs. We deeply appreciate the ongoing support of the co-trustees of the Genius Trust: James L. Alexander and Charles Slamar, Jr.

Many thanks as well to other contributors to *Evolving Planet*: James L. Alexander, Click Commerce, Inc., Illinois Department of Commerce and Economic Opportunity, Doris Kaplan and family in loving memory of Noel Kaplan, Karen Nordquist, John W. and Jeanne M. Rowe, the Arthur Rubloff Residuary Trust, U.S. Department of Education, U.S. Department of Energy, U.S. Department of Housing and Urban Development, and the many Field Museum scientists and exhibitions staff members whose work helped realize the exhibition.

The authors wish to thank Jerice Barrios, Pat Bradley, Lance Grande, Robin Groesbeck, Amy E. Harmon, Kelly Kennard, Danny LaBrecque, Matt Matcuk, David Quednau, Laura Sadler, Wendy Taylor, Todd Tubutis, and Jack Wittry. Their support and assistance were instrumental to the successful completion of this book.

Foreword

The world that we share is truly remarkable. On no other planet in this vast universe—that we know of—is there such a parade of life. From the grass that tickles our feet to the hummingbird that dazzles the eye, life's diversity is astounding. But as awesome as life is today, even more spectacular is its history.

The Field Museum's *Evolving Planet* exhibition—which opened on March 10, 2006—presents the four-billion-year history of life on Earth. Visitors come face-to-face with ancient life in the seas, spectacular flying and swimming reptiles, our early mammal ancestors, and, of course, the dinosaurs.

With the companion book to *Evolving Planet*, we bring this story home to you. We invite you to marvel at the story of our extraordinary planet, the life that calls it home, and the process that has led to life's diversity—evolution. Sharing with you the sense of awe we feel for the natural world will, we hope, motivate you to protect and conserve it as well.

On behalf of The Field Museum, I invite you to turn the page and start your four-billion-year journey.

John W. McCarter, Jr.
President and CEO
The Field Museum, Chicago

The Geologic Time Scale

QUATERNARY PERIOD | BEGAN 1.8 MILLION YEARS AGO

TODAY

TERTIARY PERIOD | BEGAN 65 MILLION YEARS AGO

CENOZOIC ERA

CRETACEOUS PERIOD | BEGAN 144 MILLION YEARS AGO

MESOZOIC ERA

JURASSIC PERIOD | BEGAN 206 MILLION YEARS AGO

TRIASSIC PERIOD | BEGAN 248 MILLION YEARS AGO

PERMIAN PERIOD | BEGAN 290 MILLION YEARS AGO

CARBONIFEROUS PERIOD | BEGAN 354 MILLION YEARS AGO

PALEOZOIC ERA

DEVONIAN PERIOD | BEGAN 417 MILLION YEARS AGO

SILURIAN PERIOD | BEGAN 443 MILLION YEARS AGO

ORDOVICIAN PERIOD | BEGAN 490 MILLION YEARS AGO

CAMBRIAN PERIOD | BEGAN 543 MILLION YEARS AGO

PRECAMBRIAN | The PRECAMBRIAN began when Earth formed 4.5 billion years ago.

Let's Take a Journey

Have you ever looked around and wondered about all the different kinds of living things? The ladybug that lands on your shirt. The tree that towers above you. The worms that appear after a rainy day. Your dog.

We share our planet with an amazing variety of life. But it's only a tiny part of the story. Of all the animals, plants, and other life-forms that have ever lived on Earth, most are now extinct. Long before all the life we see today ever came to be—from the lions of Africa to the ants of the rain forests to the bacteria that thrive in the depths of the ocean—countless other life-forms once swam, crawled, flew, or bloomed on our planet.

Like the dinosaurs, for example. Today's birds are the dinosaurs' only living descendants, so birds are actually a type of dinosaur. But most dinosaurs have been extinct for millions of years. There was gigantic *Apatosaurus*, stretching seventy-two feet long (that's almost as long as two school buses!) and weighing in at thirty-three tons. Or *Stegosaurus*, with its bizarre rows of bony plates and its spiky tail. Then later there were the woolly mammoths, with their enormous curving tusks and thick, hairy hides. Living things that seem so strange to us, it's hard to believe they ever really existed. What happened to them? What was their world like? And where did they come from in the first place?

The very first forms of life appeared on Earth a long, long time ago. Not hundreds or thousands or even millions of years ago, but four billion (4,000,000,000!) years ago. What if you could take a journey, starting when life first began on Earth, and travel through time to see for yourself how so many different types of living things came to be?

At the beginning, you'd have to look hard. All life-forms were very small—just single cells. But after billions of years, things would really get going. You'd see different life-forms sprout legs, eyes, backbones, teeth. You'd see enormous fishes, some twenty feet long, their heads protected by bony armor. You'd see spectacular sharks with rows of sharp teeth—on top of their heads. You'd see lush forests humming with the sounds of insects the size of birds. You'd see lizard-like beasts in all shapes and sizes, with flippers and sails and big bumpy heads.

Finally, after all that, you'd reach the age of dinosaurs. You'd see not only earth-shaking *Apatosaurus* and spiky *Stegosaurus* but fierce killers such as *Tyrannosaurus*, armed with massive jaws and a mouth full of teeth as sharp as steak knives. Alongside the dinosaurs, you'd watch the very first flowers bloom. You'd see the first birds take flight, sharing the skies with flying reptiles soaring on leathery wings.

You'd also come face-to-fur with the first mammals, tiny ancestors of all mammals to come. And after the last of the big dinosaurs die out, you'd watch those mammals evolve into a

◄ The earth is 4.5 billion years old! To help organize and understand this much time, scientists divide Earth's history into smaller chunks, such as eras and periods. Together, these make up the Geologic Time Scale.

wondrous variety of new forms. You'd see saber-toothed cats, and sloths as tall as a house. You'd see woolly mammoths moving in herds across the frozen plains of the ice age, breath steaming from their trunks in the chilly air. And you'd see for yourself how, among the mammals, we humans first came to live on Earth.

So how did this all happen? How does life change over time, and how did all those different forms of life come to be? As different as it all is, it's all connected, from the tiniest microbe to the most massive whale. It all came to be through evolution.

Evolution is the process of life changing over time, from generation to generation, so slowly you can't see it happening. It's the result of tiny changes adding up to bigger changes. These changes happen deep inside the cells of every living thing—in the genes, the instructions that make that living thing what it is. Genes are passed along from a parent to its offspring, and every living thing has its own unique combination. Every individual is different. Just like you are different from your parents, every generation of living thing is different, in small ways, from the last.

Over time, these small differences can add up. With enough time, they can add up to whole new forms of life. Then, with even more time, new life-forms can evolve from those life-forms. And so on. After four billion years, it adds up to an amazing diversity of life. But as evolution diversifies life, extinction wipes it out. You'll see how devastating periods of extinction—called mass extinctions—have shaped the history of life on Earth.

So how do we know about all this extinct life? Most of it we know from fossils. Fossils are the preserved remains of things that once lived. They are the clues that have helped scientists piece the story of evolution together. Around the world, in places you might never expect, people uncover fossils of plants and animals that no longer exist. Giant bones in Colorado tell us that something as big as *Apatosaurus* once lumbered across the land. Fossils found not far from the busy streets of Chicago give us a glimpse of a lush ancient forest with its giant insects and towering trees. Fossils in Africa paint us a picture of an ape-like creature—an early relative of human beings—climbing down from a tree and walking off across the grasslands in search of her next meal.

So how did it all get started? What was the very first thing to ever live on Earth—the first life-form from which everything else that has ever lived came to be?

It all began during what we call the Precambrian, which started with the actual formation of the planet! Around the sun—not long after it formed—little particles collided and stuck together in a spinning cloud of gas and dust. These particles formed clumps, which collided with other particles to form bigger clumps, and so on, until planets were formed. One of them was Earth. The earth is four and a half billion years old. Early on, it was nothing more than hot, melted rock. By four billion years ago, the outer layer of the planet cooled and rains began; the continents and oceans had been born. But it was still a very different world from what we know today. Meteorites bombarded Earth's surface. Volcanoes belched gases and lava. And the sky wasn't blue; it was orange! But on this strange planet, around four billion years ago, the very first life-form evolved: a tiny cell, so small you couldn't see it without a microscope.

We owe everything we are, all the life we see around us, to this first tiny cell. It was the ancestor of everything that has ever lived on Earth—even you.

From that first cell, other types of cells evolved. These early cells were like the bacteria we have today. Some even evolved to make their energy from the sun, like plants. And like plants they gave off oxygen, gradually turning the sky from orange to blue! Around two and a half billion years ago, a new type of cell evolved. These new cells were much different from bacteria; they were just like the cells that make up your body. From these types of cells evolved algae and the first animals. By five hundred million years ago, animals had diversified into a spectacular array of shapes and sizes. Life changed a lot in its first three and a half billion years!

The planet changed over time too. On your four-billion-year journey, you would see the continents move. You'd see oceans shrink and seas dry up, and you'd see new ones flood areas that were once dry desert. You'd sweat through millions of years of tropical warmth and shiver through long, cold ice ages. And you'd notice something. You'd notice that all of these changes to the planet itself are connected with the changes happening to life on Earth. As the planet changes, life changes.

So let's begin our journey. Let's go back five hundred million years and see some of the earliest animals. Let's see how both life and the planet itself have changed through the ages. Let's see how the human body—your body—is a result of four billion years of evolution.

Let's explore our evolving planet.

Precambrian, four billion years ago

THE Geologic TIME SCALE

TODAY

CENOZOIC ERA

QUATERNARY PERIOD
1.8 MILLION YEARS AGO
TERTIARY PERIOD

65 MILLION YEARS AGO

MESOZOIC ERA

CRETACEOUS PERIOD

144 MILLION YEARS AGO
JURASSIC PERIOD

206 MILLION YEARS AGO
TRIASSIC PERIOD

248 MILLION YEARS AGO
PERMIAN PERIOD

PALEOZOIC ERA

290 MILLION YEARS AGO
CARBONIFEROUS PERIOD

354 MILLION YEARS AGO
DEVONIAN PERIOD

417 MILLION YEARS AGO
SILURIAN PERIOD
443 MILLION YEARS AGO
ORDOVICIAN PERIOD

490 MILLION YEARS AGO
CAMBRIAN PERIOD

You are here

PRECAMBRIAN

4.5 BILLION YEARS AGO

◄ You are here: The Cambrian and Ordovician periods.

▼ Most continents are gathered in the south, and they are flooded by shallow seas.

543 MILLION YEARS AGO

Welcome to a World of Water

THE CAMBRIAN & ORDOVICIAN PERIODS
543–443 million years ago

A storm is coming. Winds howl, and the sound of thunder rumbles in the distance. But all else is silent. There is no barking of dogs. No fluttering of insects. And no rustling of leaves. The sun bakes a barren, rocky landscape. Land is lifeless.

But in the waters, something extraordinary is happening. Immense, shallow seas cover much of the ancient continents. And after more than three billion years of evolution, from the very first single cells to the very first animals and algae (plant-like organisms that use the sun's energy to make food), an "explosion" of life is taking place in these warm, shallow seas.

During the Cambrian Period, in less than thirty million years, nearly all the major animal groups living today first evolved. Ancient relatives of insects, sea stars, and corals now inhabit the seas. And among these animals, skeletons and other new features will change the shape of life forever.

Let's dive into a five-hundred-million-year-old sea and look at these sometimes bizarre—but always fascinating—animals. If you look hard enough, you'll even find one little animal that is the distant relative of not only fishes and frogs and dinosaurs, but also of you.

Cambrian Period, 505 million years ago

Animals of the Cambrian Seas

Under its hat-shaped shell, *Scenella* uses a muscular "foot" to move slowly across the seafloor. Clams and snails, squids and slugs: all are modern-day mollusks, and just like the ancient mollusk *Scenella*, they use a muscular "foot" to move or grasp their prey.

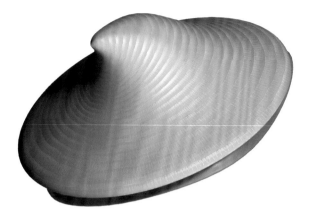

◄ *Scenella*
WIDTH: *0.3 inches*
LIVED: *505 million years ago*

Chancelloria, Capsospongia, Diagoniella, Pirania, Vauxia, and *Eiffelia* are all poriferans. You might know poriferans as sponges! Sponges don't have mouths. Instead, water carries food through tiny openings all over their bodies.

▲ *Chancelloria*
HEIGHT: *2 inches*
LIVED: *505 million years ago*

▲ *Capsospongia*
HEIGHT: *2.4 inches*
LIVED: *505 million years ago*

▲ *Diagoniella*
HEIGHT: *0.6 inches*
LIVED: *505 million years ago*

▲ *Pirania*
HEIGHT: *1.3 inches*
LIVED: *505 million years ago*

▲ *Vauxia*
HEIGHT: *1.2 inches*
LIVED: *505 million years ago*

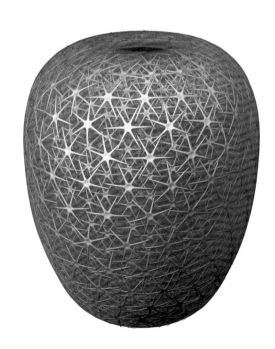

▲ *Eiffelia*
HEIGHT: *0.6 inches*
LIVED: *505 million years ago*

They may look like clams, but *Diraphora*, *Acrothyra*, *Micromitra*, and *Nisusia* are actually brachiopods. Like clams, brachiopods have two shells, but in brachiopods, one shell is slightly bigger than the other. Brachiopods are common during the Cambrian Period. Modern-day brachiopods live only in deep and cold polar waters.

▲ **Diraphora**
WIDTH: *0.4 inches*
LIVED: *505 million years ago*

▲ **Acrothyra**
WIDTH: *0.2 inches*
LIVED: *505 million years ago*

▲ **Micromitra**
WIDTH: *0.2 inches*
LIVED: *505 million years ago*

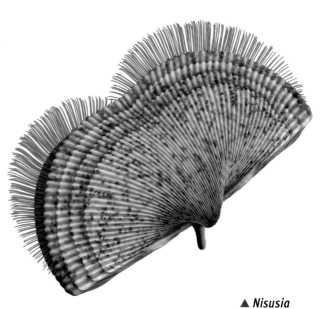

▲ **Nisusia**
WIDTH: *0.9 inches*
LIVED: *505 million years ago*

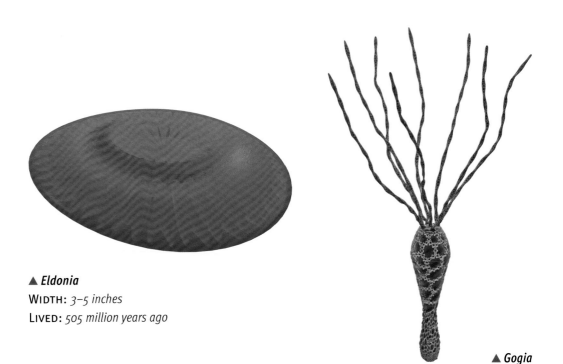

▲ **Eldonia**
WIDTH: *3–5 inches*
LIVED: *505 million years ago*

▲ **Gogia**
HEIGHT: *1.5 inches*
LIVED: *505 million years ago*

Eldonia floats high in the water. *Gogia* lives attached to the seafloor. But as different as they look and live, both are echinoderms. Think of sea urchins, sea cucumbers, and sea stars—all are modern-day echinoderms.

▶ **Pikaia**
LENGTH: *1.5 inches*
LIVED: *505 million years ago*

A funny little worm, or part of your own family tree? *Pikaia* is a chordate, and so are you! Along their backs, chordates have a nerve cord that sits on top of a tough but flexible rod called a notochord. You have a notochord as an embryo, but as you develop, a backbone forms around it. In fact, all animals with backbones—from fishes to dogs to dinosaurs—can be traced back to an animal like *Pikaia*.

◀ **Mackenzia**
HEIGHT: *3.3–6.3 inches*
LIVED: *505 million years ago*

Living on the seafloor, *Mackenzia* is similar to the sea anemones of modern seas. And like them, *Mackenzia* is a cnidarian—animals that use stinging cells to poison predators and prey. Jellyfish and corals are other types of cnidarians.

Marrella, *Odaraia*, and *Bathyuriscus* are arthropods. Like modern-day arthropods—insects, spiders, and crabs, to name a few—they have jointed legs or pincers, and they're protected by a hard outer skeleton.

Penny-size *Marrella* moves its legs to flutter just above the seafloor, stopping to rest and using its brush-like antennae to dig through the mud for food.

Odaraia swims upside down, steering with its tail and searching for food with its two enormous eyes.

Bathyuriscus is a unique type of arthropod called a trilobite. Trilobites are among the first animals with eyes. Their eyes have many small lenses that fit together like a honeycomb. Insects have the same type of eye, so trilobites probably see the world the way insects do. For the next 270 million years, trilobites will walk, dig, and swim in the seas.

When it isn't walking on the seafloor, *Canadia* can swim just above it by flapping its bristle-covered legs. *Canadia* is an annelid, the group that today includes earthworms.

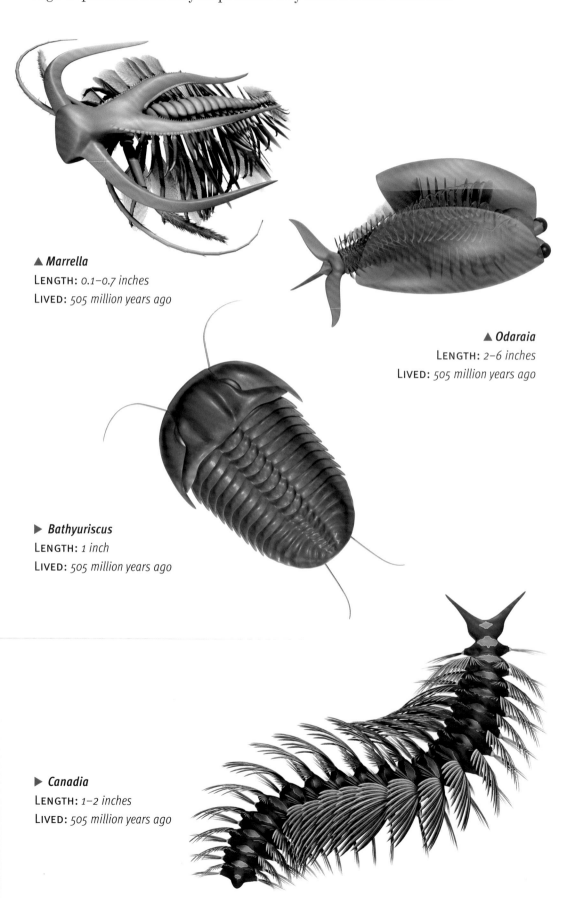

▲ *Marrella*
LENGTH: *0.1–0.7 inches*
LIVED: *505 million years ago*

▲ *Odaraia*
LENGTH: *2–6 inches*
LIVED: *505 million years ago*

▶ *Bathyuriscus*
LENGTH: *1 inch*
LIVED: *505 million years ago*

▶ *Canadia*
LENGTH: *1–2 inches*
LIVED: *505 million years ago*

What in the world?! Although these curious creatures share some features with arthropods or other animal groups, their true identities are a mystery.

Slowly crawling along the seafloor, slug-like *Wiwaxia* is covered with plated armor and has two rows of projecting spines along its back.

▶ *Wiwaxia*
LENGTH: *0.1–2.1 inches*
LIVED: *505 million years ago*

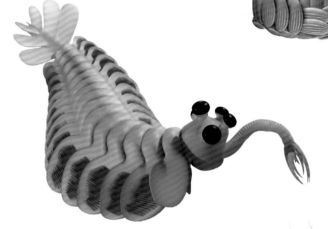

◀ *Opabinia*
LENGTH: *1.7–2.8 inches*
LIVED: *505 million years ago*

Opabinia has *five* eyes and a long, clawed "nozzle" for catching prey. Its body is lined with paddle-like lobes for swimming just above the seafloor.

▶ *Hallucigenia*
LENGTH: *0.2–1.2 inches*
LIVED: *505 million years ago*

Caterpillar-like *Hallucigenia* walks along the seafloor on seven pairs of legs, and has seven pairs of spikes along its back.

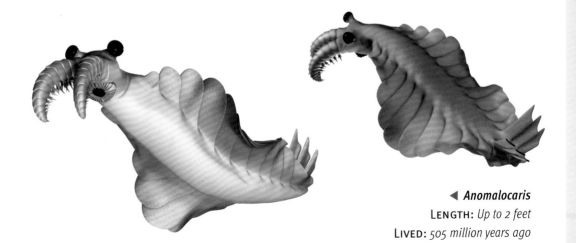

Anomalocaris is the largest predator swimming the Cambrian seas. It captures prey with two "arms" on the front of its head and then stuffs its meal into a circular mouth lined with sharp, tooth-like plates.

◀ *Anomalocaris*
LENGTH: *Up to 2 feet*
LIVED: *505 million years ago*

EVOLUTION
How It Works & How We Know
FOSSILIZATION

How do we know about life in the Cambrian Period? From fossils! Studying fossils from all periods helps scientists understand evolution—how life on Earth has changed over time.

As new animals appeared in the Cambrian seas, many new types of hard parts evolved, such as shells and plates. These hard parts form many types of skeletons. Skeletons can be inside, like yours, or outside, like a snail's shell.

Hard parts (like shells, plates, and bone) fossilize more easily than soft parts (like muscles, hair, and skin).

So, how do you become a fossil, anyway? Here are four not-so-easy steps:

STEP 1   Die.

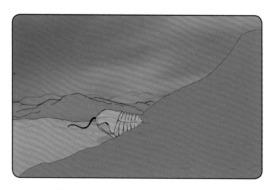

STEP 2   Get buried—fast.

If you are buried rapidly, your remains won't completely decay or be carried away by other, hungry animals. Your best bet for fast burial is to die near or in a river, lake, or ocean, where water can deposit sediment over you.

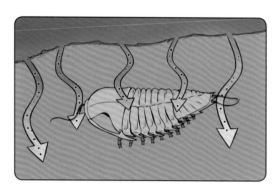

STEP 3   Soak in groundwater for a long, *looooong* time.

Groundwater contains minerals. Over time, dissolved minerals can harden after filling in cavities in your skeleton. Or the water can dissolve your skeleton, leaving only minerals in its place. Either way, your skeleton will turn to stone.

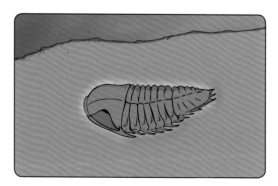

STEP 4   You'll be a fossil.

MASS EXTINCTION #1

As time passed from the Cambrian Period to the Ordovician Period, life continued to evolve. The number of animal species tripled. (A species is a group of organisms of exactly the same type, like grizzly bears, or red-winged blackbirds.) The seas were full of life! But between 465 and 443 million years ago, a mass extinction wiped out 70 percent (that's seven out of ten!) of all species. Many trilobites, brachiopods, echinoderms, and corals died.

Extinction is when a species dies out forever. Small numbers of species go extinct all the time. But when many species go extinct across much of the world, this is known as a mass extinction.

Six mass extinctions will occur by the time we finish our journey. This is the first.

What caused this first mass extinction? It's hard to know for sure, but let's see what was happening on the planet at the time. As land moved over the South Pole, ice caps formed and temperatures dropped. Perhaps many species couldn't survive the cold. Or, as water turned to ice and sea levels dropped, species that had lived in shallow seas were left high and dry.

▶ The first mass extinction lasted for around twenty-two million years at the end of the Ordovician Period.

MASS EXTINCTION #6   TODAY

CENOZOIC ERA

QUATERNARY PERIOD
1.8 MILLION YEARS AGO
TERTIARY PERIOD

65 MILLION YEARS AGO
MASS EXTINCTION #5

MESOZOIC ERA

CRETACEOUS PERIOD

144 MILLION YEARS AGO
JURASSIC PERIOD

206 MILLION YEARS AGO
MASS EXTINCTION #4
TRIASSIC PERIOD

248 MILLION YEARS AGO
MASS EXTINCTION #3

PALEOZOIC ERA

PERMIAN PERIOD

290 MILLION YEARS AGO
CARBONIFEROUS PERIOD

354 MILLION YEARS AGO
MASS EXTINCTION #2
DEVONIAN PERIOD

417 MILLION YEARS AGO
SILURIAN PERIOD

▶ MASS EXTINCTION #1

ORDOVICIAN PERIOD

490 MILLION YEARS AGO
CAMBRIAN PERIOD

543 MILLION YEARS AGO
PRECAMBRIAN

4.5 BILLION YEARS AGO

CENOZOIC ERA

QUATERNARY PERIOD
1.8 MILLION YEARS AGO

TERTIARY PERIOD

65 MILLION YEARS AGO

MESOZOIC ERA

CRETACEOUS PERIOD

144 MILLION YEARS AGO

JURASSIC PERIOD

206 MILLION YEARS AGO

TRIASSIC PERIOD

248 MILLION YEARS AGO

PERMIAN PERIOD

290 MILLION YEARS AGO

CARBONIFEROUS PERIOD

354 MILLION YEARS AGO

DEVONIAN PERIOD

417 MILLION YEARS AGO

SILURIAN PERIOD

You are here

PALEOZOIC ERA

ORDOVICIAN PERIOD

490 MILLION YEARS AGO

CAMBRIAN PERIOD

543 MILLION YEARS AGO

PRECAMBRIAN

Explore a World of Fins, Limbs, & Land Plants

THE SILURIAN & DEVONIAN PERIODS
443–354 million years ago

◀ You are here: The Silurian and Devonian periods.

▼ Continents that once were separate have come together along the equator and in the Southern Hemisphere.

443 MILLION YEARS AGO

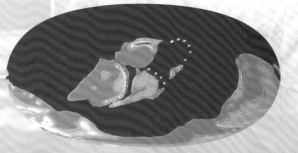

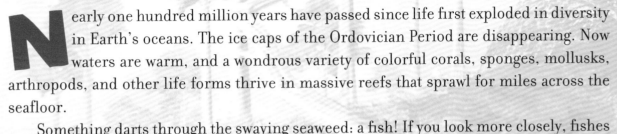

Nearly one hundred million years have passed since life first exploded in diversity in Earth's oceans. The ice caps of the Ordovician Period are disappearing. Now waters are warm, and a wondrous variety of colorful corals, sponges, mollusks, arthropods, and other life forms thrive in massive reefs that sprawl for miles across the seafloor.

Something darts through the swaying seaweed: a fish! If you look more closely, fishes are everywhere. There are fishes with delicate fins and fishes with fins that are sharp and spiny. Some are small and scaly with suckers for mouths. Others are more than twenty feet long and covered in bony armor, with fierce jaws that can kill with a single snapping bite.

Meanwhile, on land, something entirely new is happening. Earth's barren landscape is turning green. The first land plants have evolved. They started out small and moss-like at the water's edge as some types of green algae evolved new ways of living on land. Slowly, these little trailblazers have given way to new plants with leaves and woody trunks, plants that are able to survive ever farther inland. The lifeless, rocky landscape is growing lush with new forest.

Back at the shoreline, there's more big news. Remember those fishes? Some of them have evolved stumpy fins that they use for "walking" through the shallow, swampy waters. Among them, some new animals have evolved that are not really fish anymore at all. They have limbs, and they can take their first steps onto land.

Devonian Period, 370 million years ago

A Diversity of Fishes Swims the Seas

Remember *Pikaia*, that little creature from the Cambrian seas with the nerve cord running down its back? Over the last few million years, other new life-forms have evolved from a creature like *Pikaia*. These new life-forms have that same nerve cord that their ancestors had. But around that nerve cord, there's something new: a backbone!

These new life-forms are vertebrates: animals with backbones. A backbone is a good thing to have. It's a great place for muscles to attach, helping an animal move, and it helps support an animal's weight.

These first vertebrates are the very first fishes.

But some of these fishes probably look like nothing you've ever seen before. The Silurian and Devonian periods are an amazing time in the oceans, with fishes evolving into a wondrous variety of new forms.

Like many of the very earliest fishes, *Protaspis* is well protected by a bony shield covering its head. There's something else that makes early fishes like *Protaspis* different from all the other fishes here: It doesn't have jaws. It has a mouth, but it can't open wide to take a big bite. It eats by sucking in its prey.

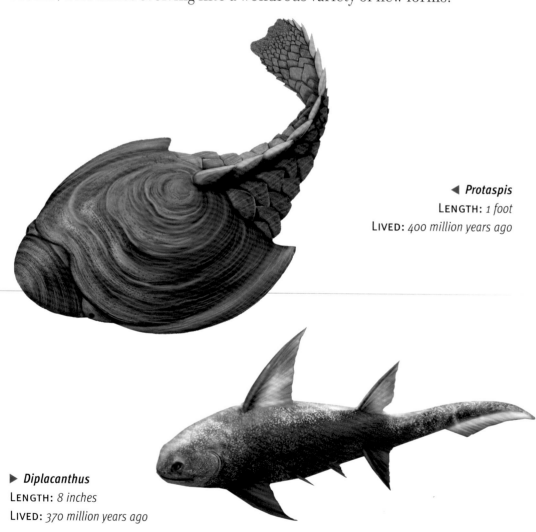

◀ *Protaspis*
LENGTH: *1 foot*
LIVED: *400 million years ago*

Diplacanthus has some interesting fins. If you could touch them, their front edges would feel firm and spiny, like long, curved thorns. You won't see any modern-day fishes like *Diplacanthus*, but fishes with this type of fin are everywhere in Devonian rivers and seas.

▶ *Diplacanthus*
LENGTH: *8 inches*
LIVED: *370 million years ago*

◀ Coccosteus
LENGTH: *1 foot*
LIVED: *375 million years ago*

With their heads covered by bony plates, *Coccosteus* and *Dunkleosteus* are well-protected predators. *Dunkleosteus* is especially fearsome—it can grow to be twenty feet long, with a bite that could crack concrete! With tooth-like plates of bone on those powerful jaws, this fish rules the Devonian seas.

▼ Dunkleosteus
LENGTH: *20 feet*
LIVED: *375 million years ago*

◀ Palaeoniscum
LENGTH: *8 inches*
LIVED: *250 million years ago*

Of all the fishes here, *Palaeoniscum* may look the most familiar to you. That's because most fishes living in the modern world—from goldfish to salmon to tuna to sturgeon—are its close relatives. You can tell from its fins. The delicate fins most modern fishes have, with their thin skin and fine bones, are the same type of fins found on this Paleozoic fish.

Life Makes the Move to Land

Let's take a peek up above the water. While the oceans teem with life, the planet has been quietly transformed. That desolate landscape is long gone. In its place are dense mosses, spindly stems, coiling fern-like fronds. Horsetails cluster at the water's edge, their narrow leaves growing in rings around long shoots. Trees with scaly trunks tower over a forest floor that is newly lush and green.

Land plants have evolved. Their ancestors are algae that colonized the shoreline. Like algae, the first land plants lived in wet areas, where water bathed them in the nutrients the plants needed to survive. But new types of land plants evolved special stems that hold and transport water and nutrients. Stems also allow plants to stand up and grow taller. Some of these plants have evolved to be woody trees, which can grow really tall. Roots let plants draw water from deep in the ground, so they don't need to be near the water's edge. And while algae and the very first land plants needed water to reproduce, some of these newer plants have pollen and seeds, which let them reproduce just about anywhere.

▲ Forests of Devonian time

Life Takes Its First Steps

There's a rustle in the plants at the water's edge. Something is moving. A fish? No, it's moving on land. An insect? Insects have lived in these forests for a few million years now (they evolved back in the Silurian Period from other types of arthropods that invaded land soon after plants). But no, it's too big to be an insect. It's something new. It's a tetrapod.

A tetrapod is a vertebrate that has four limbs (arms and legs) and digits (fingers and toes). You are a tetrapod. This little tetrapod is another one of your very early ancestors. So where did it come from?

Over the last few million years, one type of fish evolved to have muscular, fleshy fins. Some of these fleshy-finned fishes evolved ways of using their special fins to "walk" and push their way through the dense, swampy growth in shallow waters. Over time, the fins of some of these "walking" fishes evolved into limbs with digits. The first tetrapods have come ashore.

Life on Earth will never be the same.

Tiktaalik, which lived around 375 million years ago, is a "missing link" between fishes and tetrapods. It has a long, fishy tail, but its front fins are limb-like. It also has nostrils, which means it can breathe air. If you are going to live on land, you need to be able to breathe air!

▲ *Tiktaalik*
LENGTH: *9 feet*
LIVED: *375 million years ago*

Acanthostega, which lived around 360 million years ago, is an early tetrapod. It's still fish-like. But instead of fins, it has four feet. And those feet have digits—eight of them, in fact!

◀ *Acanthostega*
LENGTH: *2 feet*
LIVED: *360 million years ago*

MASS EXTINCTION #2

It's the end of the Devonian Period, around 360 million years ago. Mass extinction has struck Earth for the second time.

Just like the first mass extinction almost 100 million years earlier, seven out of every ten species in the oceans have been wiped out. Remember those fishes with the bony heads? They are all gone. So are many types of corals, mollusks, and trilobites. The magnificent reefs that grew so large during the Devonian Period have been devastated.

Exactly what happened and caused this loss of life isn't clear. One thing is certain: Continents are clustered over the South Pole again. Could this be part of the problem? The pole is cold year-round. So now when it snows, the snowfall accumulates on land.

This buildup of snow forms glaciers, which grow as they freeze, using up more and more water from Earth's oceans. When this water freezes, sea levels drop. With lower sea levels, life in the shallower oceans might not have been able to survive. Their habitat may have disappeared.

Changes on the planet are connected to changes in life on Earth. As the continents move, it can change the environment in which species live. Not everything will survive.

▶ The second mass extinction lasted for around ten million years at the end of the Devonian Period.

Timeline

CENOZOIC ERA

MASS EXTINCTION #6   TODAY
QUATERNARY PERIOD
1.8 MILLION YEARS AGO
TERTIARY PERIOD
65 MILLION YEARS AGO
MASS EXTINCTION #5

MESOZOIC ERA

CRETACEOUS PERIOD
144 MILLION YEARS AGO
JURASSIC PERIOD
206 MILLION YEARS AGO
MASS EXTINCTION #4
TRIASSIC PERIOD
248 MILLION YEARS AGO
MASS EXTINCTION #3

PALEOZOIC ERA

PERMIAN PERIOD
290 MILLION YEARS AGO
CARBONIFEROUS PERIOD

▶ **MASS EXTINCTION #2**
DEVONIAN PERIOD
417 MILLION YEARS AGO
SILURIAN PERIOD
443 MILLION YEARS AGO
MASS EXTINCTION #1
ORDOVICIAN PERIOD
490 MILLION YEARS AGO
CAMBRIAN PERIOD
543 MILLION YEARS AGO
PRECAMBRIAN

4.5 BILLION YEARS AGO

The Geologic
Time Scale

TODAY

QUATERNARY Period
1.8 MILLION YEARS AGO
TERTIARY Period

CENOZOIC ERA

65 MILLION YEARS AGO
CRETACEOUS Period

144 MILLION YEARS AGO
JURASSIC Period

MESOZOIC ERA

206 MILLION YEARS AGO
TRIASSIC Period

248 MILLION YEARS AGO
PERMIAN Period

290 MILLION YEARS AGO
CARBONIFEROUS Period

You are here

DEVONIAN Period

PALEOZOIC ERA

417 MILLION YEARS AGO
SILURIAN Period

443 MILLION YEARS AGO
ORDOVICIAN Period

490 MILLION YEARS AGO
CAMBRIAN Period

543 MILLION YEARS AGO
PRECAMBRIAN

4.5 BILLION YEARS AGO

◄ You are here: The Carboniferous Period.

▼ A cluster of continents stretches almost pole-to-pole.

354 MILLION YEARS AGO

Step into a Warm World of Swampy Forests & Spectacular Sharks

THE CARBONIFEROUS PERIOD
354–290 million years ago

Though ice still covers the South Pole, the continents closer to the equator are tropical and warm. Steamy, swampy forests hum with life. There are dragonflies the size of model airplanes, and three-foot-long millipedes with dozens of legs. Little four-footed tetrapods scurry up tree trunks and hop from log to log. They look like salamanders, leaving tiny footprints on the muddy ground, sometimes causing a splash as they jump into the swamp for a swim.

And not everything in the seas died during the second mass extinction. One group of fishes that survived is having its heyday: sharks! They are the fiercest predators in the oceans—and some of the strangest.

Carboniferous Period, 310 million years ago

Sensational Sharks
Patrol the Deep

Believe it or not, these strange-looking sharks aren't such a strange sight in the Carboniferous seas. The Carboniferous is an amazing time for sharks, which are more diverse than they have ever been before.

Sharks are a unique group of fishes that have skeletons made of cartilage. Your ears and the tip of your nose are made of cartilage. It's more flexible than bone. But sharks' teeth aren't made of cartilage—most sharks are fierce predators, with the sharp teeth to prove it. Some of these sharks even have "teeth" in unusual places!

Tiny *Bandringa* is only about five inches long—and almost half of that is its long snout! But eel-like *Orodus* can grow to be twenty-five feet long. Carboniferous sharks come in all shapes and sizes!

▶ *Bandringa*
LENGTH: *5 inches*
LIVED: *310 million years ago*

◀ *Orodus*
LENGTH: *25 feet*
LIVED: *310 million years ago*

Helicoprion has a coiled spiral of teeth hanging from its lower jaw. What could that be for? Perhaps the shark charges into a school of fish when it wants to feed and thrashes this spiky tool about, snagging its prey. These sharks have some mysterious features!

▶ **Helicoprion**
LENGTH: *4 feet*
LIVED: *300 million years ago*

▶ **Stethacanthus**
LENGTH: *5 feet*
LIVED: *340 million years ago*

Stethacanthus is even more of a mystery. This shark has a platform growing out of its back fin, covered with pointed, tooth-like scales. The same scales cover the top of its head. Do these oddly placed "teeth" make the shark look fierce? Do they attract mates? To know for sure, we'd have to hang around in the Carboniferous and watch this shark in action!

◀ **Symmorium**
LENGTH: *4 feet*
LIVED: *310 million years ago*

Not all Carboniferous sharks are oddballs. *Symmorium* would look right at home in the seas of the modern world. Sharks are one of evolution's greatest success stories. They've been around for hundreds of millions of years, and while some unusual forms have come and gone, they haven't had to change much to survive.

Forests Cover the Continents

Mist hangs in the warm air. The scent of decaying leaves rises from the forest floor. Ferns grow everywhere, some as tall as trees, their delicate fronds coiling in spirals. Even taller than the ferns are towering trees—some as tall as a fifteen-story building!—with straight, scaly trunks topped with leafy branches. Cones from these trees carpet the ground. Fallen logs provide places for salamander-like tetrapods to hide and wait for their next meal—an unlucky insect—to happen by. Everywhere, the ground seems soggy, steeped in the waters of nearby swamps and lagoons where jellyfish float and shrimp-like creatures burrow in the mud. The air is alive with the whir of dragonflies' wings, the rustle of leaves, the sounds of forest life.

How Do We Know So Much About the Carboniferous World?

A Fabulous Fossil Site:
Mazon Creek, Illinois, USA

Let's travel forward to our own time, just for a moment, and pay a visit to an interesting place. Not far from the city of Chicago, Illinois, some of the best fossils of Carboniferous plants and animals in the world can be found. Called Mazon Creek, the spot is known for its coal mines. (Coal mining is how many of the Mazon Creek fossils were found; miners dug for coal, and found fossils.) But 310 million years ago this same place was covered for miles in swampy forests, rivers, and shallow bays.

◀ Giant insects buzz through an Illinois forest, 310 million years ago.

When plants and animals in these forests died, the rivers carried them into the bays, where fine sediments quickly buried them before they could decay. They left spectacular fossils: Coiled fern fronds, insects' wings, leaves, seeds, and tree bark. These fossils give scientists a glimpse of an ancient world and teach them about how the planet has changed over millions of years.

▶ Tree fern frond (*Pecopteris*)
LENGTH: *10 inches*
LIVED: *310 million years ago*

▶ Part of a seed fern frond
(*Neuropteris*)
LENGTH: *4 inches*
LIVED: *310 million years ago*

▶ Horsetail trunk (*Calamites*)
HEIGHT: *6 inches*
LIVED: *310 million years ago*

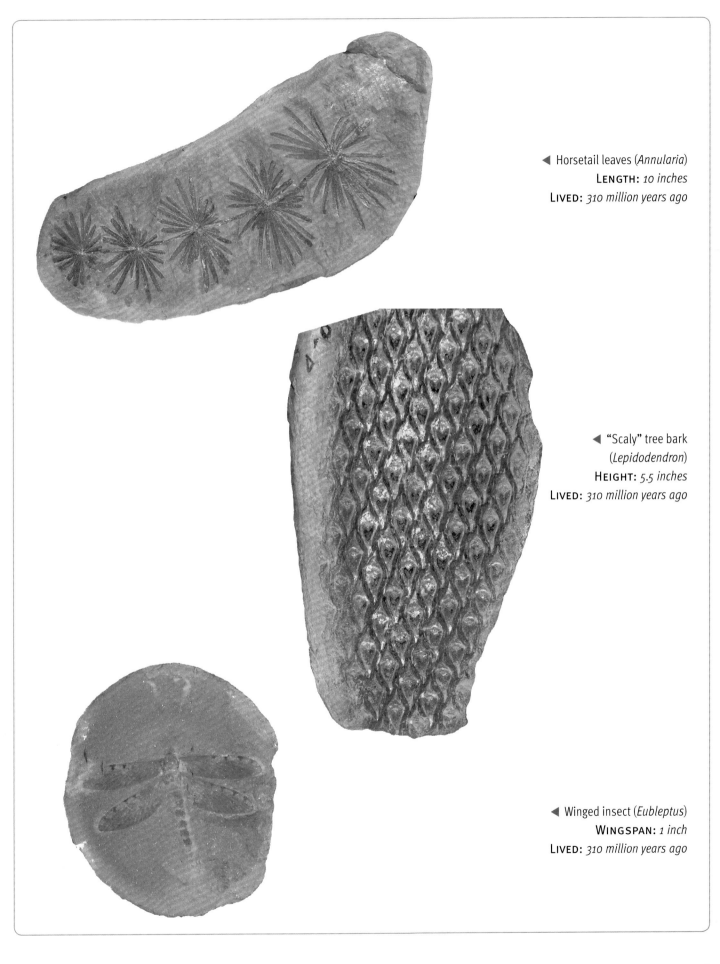

◄ Horsetail leaves (*Annularia*)
LENGTH: *10 inches*
LIVED: *310 million years ago*

◄ "Scaly" tree bark
(*Lepidodendron*)
HEIGHT: *5.5 inches*
LIVED: *310 million years ago*

◄ Winged insect (*Eubleptus*)
WINGSPAN: *1 inch*
LIVED: *310 million years ago*

The Geologic Time Scale

TODAY

CENOZOIC ERA

QUATERNARY PERIOD
1.8 MILLION YEARS AGO
TERTIARY PERIOD

65 MILLION YEARS AGO

MESOZOIC ERA

CRETACEOUS PERIOD

144 MILLION YEARS AGO
JURASSIC PERIOD

206 MILLION YEARS AGO
TRIASSIC PERIOD

248 MILLION YEARS AGO
PERMIAN PERIOD

You are here

PALEOZOIC ERA

CARBONIFEROUS PERIOD

354 MILLION YEARS AGO
DEVONIAN PERIOD

417 MILLION YEARS AGO
SILURIAN PERIOD
443 MILLION YEARS AGO
ORDOVICIAN PERIOD

490 MILLION YEARS AGO
CAMBRIAN PERIOD

543 MILLION YEARS AGO
PRECAMBRIAN

4.5 BILLION YEARS AGO

◀ You are here: The Permian Period.

▼ The continents have assembled into one giant landmass: Pangaea.

290 MILLION YEARS AGO

Sail Backs & Supercontinents

THE PERMIAN PERIOD
290–248 million years ago

Yesterday's hunt was not a success. Perched atop a rocky cliff, two great sail backs absorb the morning's sun. Their hunger grows. Below, giant amphibians follow their daily routine. Some cruise through the river's waters; others munch plants on land. The sail backs are watching. Now warm, they rise from their bellies, stretch their legs, and begin creeping down to the river. It's time to feed.

Welcome to the Permian Period. The great swampy forests of the Carboniferous are no more. All the continents have drifted together, and a giant supercontinent—Pangaea—has formed. On this vast landmass, a patchwork of different environments can be found, from dry deserts to lush forests.

Tetrapods thrive in this new world. They have evolved new forms and new ways of living. Among the sail backs and amphibians, early reptiles scamper about. If you look carefully, you may just find the early relatives of dinosaurs and mammals—including you.

But in thirty million years, at the end of the Permian Period, life will be changed forever: Life will almost completely die.

Permian Period, 280 million years ago

Frogs & Salamanders Are No Match for These Amphibians

A head shaped like an airplane's wings? Bony armor for protection? Six feet long and one hundred pounds?! The amphibians of the Permian have evolved all kinds of shapes and sizes. But like frogs, salamanders, and other modern-day amphibians, they probably live close to rivers or lakes or swamps, where they can lay their soft eggs in water.

▲ *Eryops*
LENGTH: *6 feet*
LIVED: *280 million years ago*

With their sharp, cone-shaped teeth, *Eryops* and *Acheloma* are meat eaters. *Eryops* probably spends most of its time in the water, but with a very strong backbone to help support its weight, *Acheloma* is adapted for hunting on land.

◀ *Acheloma*
LENGTH: *3 feet*
LIVED: *280 million years ago*

▶ Cacops
LENGTH: *1.5 feet*
LIVED: *280 million years ago*

It's tough living alongside big meat eaters. If you're not careful, you could become dinner! Little *Cacops*—a meat eater itself—has a row of bony armor along its back to help protect it.

◀ Pantylus
LENGTH: *1 foot*
LIVED: *280 million years ago*

Pantylus has dozens of blunt teeth lining its jaws and the roof of its mouth. Teeth like this are good for eating snails or other animals with hard shells.

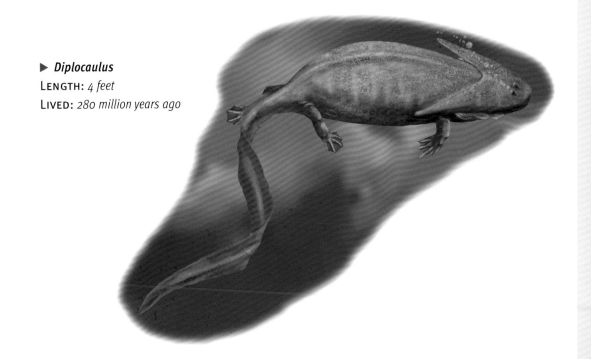

▶ Diplocaulus
LENGTH: *4 feet*
LIVED: *280 million years ago*

Like the wings of an airplane, the boomerang-shaped head of *Diplocaulus* provides "lift" in the water. Tilting its head up, it rises to the surface. Tilting its head down, it can take a dive.

Seymouria is a world traveler! East to west, it can be found across Pangaea. With all of the continents connected as one giant landmass, some animals travel far and wide.

▲ *Seymouria*
LENGTH: *3 feet*
LIVED: *280 million years ago*

Diadectes is a common sight in early Permian times. It's also one of the oldest known plant-eating tetrapods. Its long front teeth are good for snipping leafy bites, and molar-like back teeth are good for grinding food to a pulp.

▼ *Diadectes*
LENGTH: *6 feet*
LIVED: *280 million years ago*

A Good Egg

A new type of tetrapod has evolved: amniotes. Unlike amphibians, whose eggs would dry out if not laid in water, amniotes have eggs that are more resistant to drying out. With their new eggs, amniotes are not tied to the water, so they have spread far and wide across Pangaea. As they have evolved, they've split into two groups: reptiles and synapsids. Let's meet these early amniotes. But look carefully. You're about to meet the ancient relatives of not only dinosaurs and crocodiles, but also the ancient relatives of you and all other mammals too!

Bradysaurus is one of the biggest reptiles of the Permian. But this giant is gentle. Inside its jaws are leaf-shaped teeth, good for cropping leafy bites.

▲ *Bradysaurus* (reptile)
LENGTH: *8 feet*
LIVED: *250 million years ago*

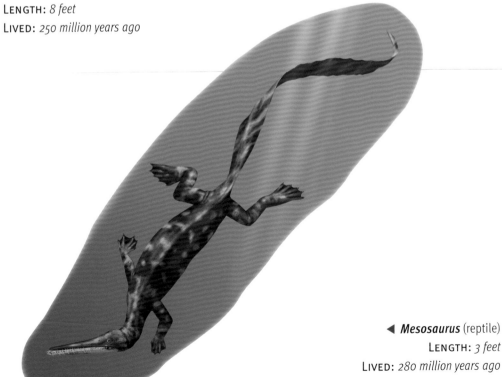

With its long, flat tail and paddle-shaped feet, *Mesosaurus* is a champion swimmer. Though reptiles do not need to be in the water for egg laying, there is food to be found in the waters! Over time, many reptiles will become swimmers. *Mesosaurus* is among the first.

◀ *Mesosaurus* (reptile)
LENGTH: *3 feet*
LIVED: *280 million years ago*

Reptiles & Synapsids: What's the Difference?

There are many differences throughout their skeletons, but one of the most obvious is all about the holes in their heads. What are these openings for? It's tough to tell, but they may allow more room for jaw muscles to expand when the mouth closes.

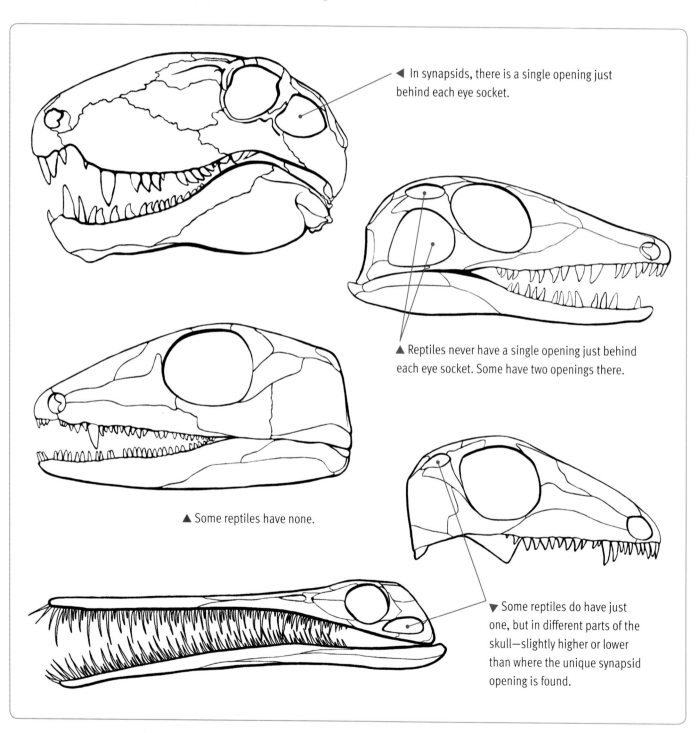

◀ In synapsids, there is a single opening just behind each eye socket.

▲ Reptiles never have a single opening just behind each eye socket. Some have two openings there.

▲ Some reptiles have none.

▼ Some reptiles do have just one, but in different parts of the skull—slightly higher or lower than where the unique synapsid opening is found.

▲ **Captorhinus** (reptile)
LENGTH: *8 inches*
LIVED: *280 million years ago*

Captorhinus and *Labidosaurus* are very close relatives. Both have hooked snouts and heart-shaped heads. And both have rows and rows of teeth with sharp ridges, good for eating insects or other small animals.

▲ **Labidosaurus** (reptile)
LENGTH: *3.5 feet*
LIVED: *280 million years ago*

▲ **Protorothyris** (reptile)
LENGTH: *1.5 feet*
LIVED: *285 million years ago*

Its pointy teeth make little *Protorothyris* well adapted for catching insects. Though it looks like a lizard of the modern world, *Protorothyris* is actually one of the oldest types of reptiles.

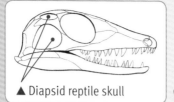

▲ Diapsid reptile skull

Youngina is a special type of reptile called a diapsid. Diapsids have two openings in the skull behind each eye socket. Other diapsids? The crocodiles, lizards, snakes, and turtles back in the modern world. And dinosaurs! All of them can be traced back to a diapsid ancestor like tiny *Youngina*.

▲ *Youngina* (reptile)
LENGTH: *1.5 feet*
LIVED: *250 million years ago*

Long legs make *Varanops* a speedy hunter. And its sharp, curved, pointed teeth are perfect for tearing flesh!

▲ *Varanops* (synapsid)
LENGTH: *3.5 feet*
LIVED: *280 million years ago*

Casea may have a small head, but it has a big gut! The spoon-shaped teeth along its jaws are good for shredding leaves and stems. And its large digestive system is good for breaking down tough plants.

▲ *Casea* (synapsid)
LENGTH: *4 feet*
LIVED: *280 million years ago*

◄ *Dimetrodon* (synapsid)
LENGTH: *12 feet*
LIVED: *280 million years ago*

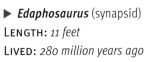

► *Edaphosaurus* (synapsid)
LENGTH: *11 feet*
LIVED: *280 million years ago*

Both *Dimetrodon* and *Edaphosaurus* have long spines on their backbone. Covered in skin, the spines form a great sail on their backs. But with its many blunt teeth, *Edaphosaurus* is a plant eater. *Dimetrodon* has a mouth full of sharp daggers. It's one of the top meat eaters of its day.

◄ *Ophiacodon* (synapsid)
LENGTH: *5 feet*
LIVED: *280 million years ago*

Living along lakeshores and riverbanks, *Ophiacodon* uses the pointy teeth along its long snout to snag fish for its dinner.

The sharp, saber-like teeth of *Lycaenops* can easily puncture and tear through flesh. As we'll see along our journey, long saber teeth evolve many times in Earth's long history. They must be very useful for a predator.

▶ *Lycaenops* (synapsid)
LENGTH: *3 feet*
LIVED: *250 million years ago*

Jonkeria is one of the largest synapsids of the Permian. But don't be afraid; this giant is a plant eater. It also has a thick skull, good for head-butting— just as a modern-day ram uses its horns to defend its territory or attract a mate.

◀ *Jonkeria* (synapsid)
LENGTH: *12 feet*
LIVED: *250 million years ago*

Its sharp, turtle-like beak helps *Aulacephalodon* snip plants, and its large gut helps it digest tough plant matter. It might use its tusks for defense, or to attract mates.

▶ *Aulacephalodon* (synapsid)
LENGTH: *7 feet*
LIVED: *250 million years ago*

Looking at tiny *Thrinaxodon*, you are actually looking at your own family tree. *Thrinaxodon* is a special type of synapsid called a cynodont. How are you related to cynodonts? As we continue our journey in time, you'll see mammals evolving from a cynodont like *Thrinaxodon*.

◀ *Thrinaxodon* (synapsid)
LENGTH: *1.5 feet*
LIVED: *245 million years ago*

MASS EXTINCTION #3

Life has been around on Earth for almost four billion years. But now, at the end of the Permian Period, life is almost completely wiped out.

This mass extinction is the most devastating mass extinction in Earth's history. Over 90 percent of animals in the seas and oceans become extinct. On land, 80 percent of animals suffer extinction.

Why did nearly all animal life on Earth die out? As with the last two mass extinctions, the cause is not clear. But there are clues. In some parts of the world, massive volcanic eruptions have been releasing enormous quantities of lava and gases for many, many years. These gases trap heat in the atmosphere, causing temperatures to warm around the world. Did global warming cause the worst mass extinction the planet has ever seen?

MASS EXTINCTION #6	TODAY
QUATERNARY PERIOD	
1.8 MILLION YEARS AGO	
TERTIARY PERIOD	CENOZOIC ERA
65 MILLION YEARS AGO	
MASS EXTINCTION #5	
CRETACEOUS PERIOD	
144 MILLION YEARS AGO	
JURASSIC PERIOD	MESOZOIC ERA
206 MILLION YEARS AGO	
MASS EXTINCTION #4	
TRIASSIC PERIOD	
▶ MASS EXTINCTION #3	
PERMIAN PERIOD	
290 MILLION YEARS AGO	
CARBONIFEROUS PERIOD	
354 MILLION YEARS AGO	
MASS EXTINCTION #2	
DEVONIAN PERIOD	PALEOZOIC ERA
417 MILLION YEARS AGO	
SILURIAN PERIOD	
443 MILLION YEARS AGO	
MASS EXTINCTION #1	
ORDOVICIAN PERIOD	
490 MILLION YEARS AGO	
CAMBRIAN PERIOD	
543 MILLION YEARS AGO	
PRECAMBRIAN	
4.5 BILLION YEARS AGO	

▶ The third mass extinction lasted only one million years, between 251 and 250 million years ago, but it was the most devastating in Earth's history.

EVOLUTION
How It Works & How We Know
NATURAL SELECTION

Single-celled bacteria. Little worm-like chordates in the oceans. Sponges. Arthropods. Mollusks. Algae. Plants. Fishes. Amphibians. Reptiles.

We've seen life go through some tremendous changes since it first evolved on Earth almost four billion years ago. How did all these changes happen? What's behind this incredible diversity?

It's called natural selection.

It's pretty simple, really. When an individual of a species has features that make it more likely to survive, it's more likely to reproduce, passing on to its young the genes for the features that helped it to survive. This means that its offspring will also be more likely to survive. Natural selection: By their nature, some individuals are "selected" to survive.

Over time, these small changes add up to big changes: new species. Then new species evolve from *those* species. With enough time, it all adds up to a planet with an astounding variety of life.

So how does it work?

In any group of organisms of the same species, there is variation. Think about your own family and friends. You are all the same species, but you are all unique; you all look different. This is true of every species on Earth.

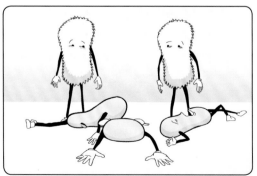

◄ Imagine, for example, a group of the same species in which some individuals have longer legs than others. Now imagine that something in their environment changes. Suppose a new predator appears. The individuals with longer legs can more easily outrun the predator.

These longer-legged individuals are better suited to their environment, so they are the ones that survive. When they reproduce, they pass on to their offspring the genes that made them long-legged. Over many generations, this adds up to a group with more long-legged individuals than short-legged ones.

◄ Let's take another example—say, a group with some individuals that have more hair than others. Now imagine that the climate changes: It gets colder. The hairier individuals are now better suited to survive the cold. Eventually, this adds up to a group with mostly hairy individuals.

With enough changes like these—and enough time—a group of organisms can become so different from their ancestors that they are a whole new species.

New predators, new climates—the thing about natural selection is, it's all about the surrounding environment. No trait, in itself, is good or bad. It's just that the trait either helps an individual to survive in its environment, or it doesn't.

And the environment is always changing. The continents are always moving, making the climate warmer and colder, introducing new species into new places. As the planet changes, life changes.

Stick around, and we'll see how natural selection will drive the evolution of life on our planet over the next 250 million years.

Charles Darwin Gave "Natural Selection" Its Name

▲ Charles Darwin

As long as humans have lived on Earth, we have looked around us and wondered at the diversity of life on our planet. Different scientists and thinkers have tried to provide an explanation. Charles Darwin was the first one to get it right.

Darwin was born in England in 1809. At the age of twenty-two, Darwin—an observant nature lover with some scientific training—was asked to join the crew of the HMS *Beagle* on a voyage to explore the coast of South America and its nearby islands. Along the way, Darwin collected and studied the animals, plants, and fossils he encountered. In comparing the living and extinct life-forms he observed, he noted similarities and differences that got him thinking.

After the *Beagle* returned to England, Darwin studied the specimens he had collected and made observations for more than twenty years, turning his ideas over in his mind. Finally, he arrived at his theory about how all this diversity of life had come to be. In 1859, Darwin published *On the Origin of Species by Means of Natural Selection*, a book in which he described the process by which individuals better suited to their environment survive to pass these traits along to their offspring, eventually resulting in new species.

So, what is a theory? In science, a theory is not simply a hunch, or a best guess, or something that just seems to make sense. For an explanation to be a scientific theory, it must be an explanation that is supported by evidence, and it must repeatedly stand up when put to the test.

The theory of evolution by means of natural selection is one of the most important discoveries in the history of science. Thanks to Darwin, scientists today—studying everything from fossils to DNA to living plants and animals to our own human bodies—understand how evolution works.

The Geologic
Time Scale

CENOZOIC ERA

QUATERNARY PERIOD
1.8 MILLION YEARS AGO
TERTIARY PERIOD

TODAY

65 MILLION YEARS AGO

CRETACEOUS PERIOD

MESOZOIC ERA

144 MILLION YEARS AGO

JURASSIC PERIOD

206 MILLION YEARS AGO

TRIASSIC PERIOD

You are here

PERMIAN PERIOD

PALEOZOIC ERA

290 MILLION YEARS AGO

CARBONIFEROUS PERIOD

354 MILLION YEARS AGO

DEVONIAN PERIOD

417 MILLION YEARS AGO

SILURIAN PERIOD

443 MILLION YEARS AGO

ORDOVICIAN PERIOD

490 MILLION YEARS AGO

CAMBRIAN PERIOD

543 MILLION YEARS AGO

PRECAMBRIAN

◀ You are here: The Triassic, Jurassic, and Cretaceous periods.

▼ The supercontinent Pangaea reaches its largest size during the Triassic Period, then later begins to break apart during the Jurassic.

248 MILLION YEARS AGO

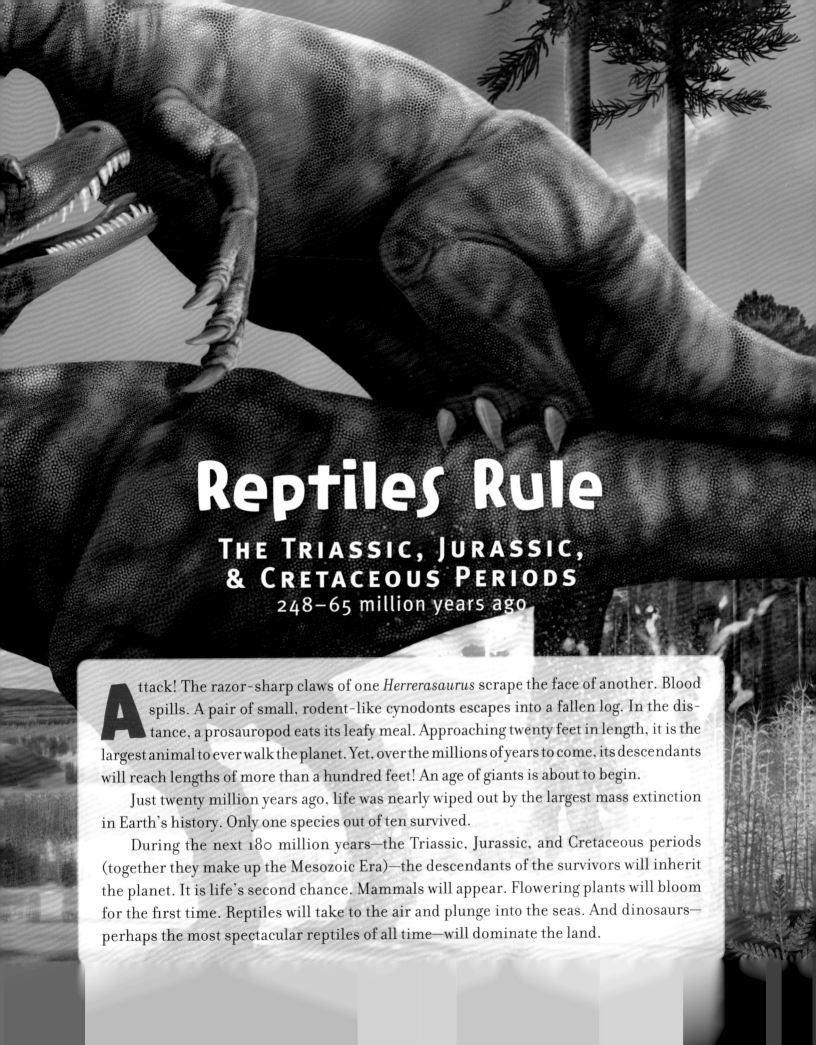

Reptiles Rule

THE TRIASSIC, JURASSIC, & CRETACEOUS PERIODS
248–65 million years ago

Attack! The razor-sharp claws of one *Herrerasaurus* scrape the face of another. Blood spills. A pair of small, rodent-like cynodonts escapes into a fallen log. In the distance, a prosauropod eats its leafy meal. Approaching twenty feet in length, it is the largest animal to ever walk the planet. Yet, over the millions of years to come, its descendants will reach lengths of more than a hundred feet! An age of giants is about to begin.

Just twenty million years ago, life was nearly wiped out by the largest mass extinction in Earth's history. Only one species out of ten survived.

During the next 180 million years—the Triassic, Jurassic, and Cretaceous periods (together they make up the Mesozoic Era)—the descendants of the survivors will inherit the planet. It is life's second chance. Mammals will appear. Flowering plants will bloom for the first time. Reptiles will take to the air and plunge into the seas. And dinosaurs— perhaps the most spectacular reptiles of all time—will dominate the land.

Mammals:
A Humble Beginning

Remember *Dimetrodon* and *Lycaenops*? Synapsids were a very common sight during the Permian Period. But only a handful survived the great mass extinction at the end of the period. One group that did survive was the cynodonts. And it's lucky for you that they did. If cynodonts like *Thrinaxodon* hadn't survived, you wouldn't be here!

◀ *Dimetrodon*

▶ *Lycaenops*

◀ *Thrinaxodon*

During the Triassic Period, cynodonts became more and more mammal-like. Some evolved hair and special teeth such as incisors (for biting) and canines (for tearing). Eventually, around 220 million years ago, we see the first mammals evolve from them.

These early mammals are all very small. And they will stay small for the next 150 million years, living in the shadows of the dinosaurs. The biggest will be barely bigger than a modern-day house cat!

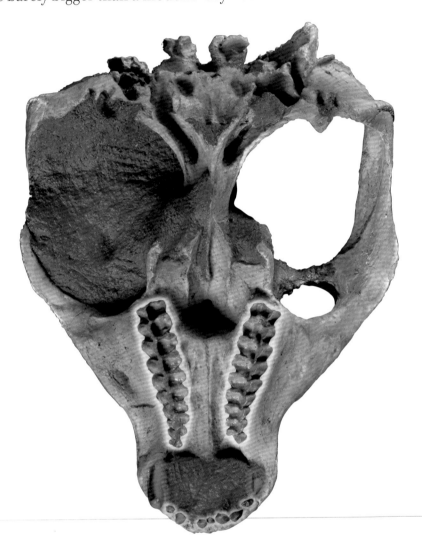

On this cynodont skull, you can see incisors at the very front (green), pointy canines right behind them (orange), and cheek teeth in the back (yellow).

◀ *Morganucodon*
LENGTH: *3 inches*
LIVED: *210 million years ago*

With its large eyes and a long snout, little *Morganucodon* has keen vision and a good sense of smell, good for hunting at night.

EVOLUTION
How It Works & How We Know
PHYLOGENY

So, how *do* we know where mammals come from? In other words, how do we know the evolutionary history—or phylogeny—of mammals?

By comparing them to all other living things. Organisms that share more features are more closely related, so scientists can tell how organisms are related by looking at their features.

Let's start with animals that have backbones.

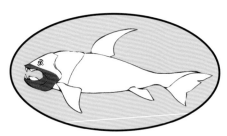

STEP 1   Some of the creatures with backbones also have jaws.

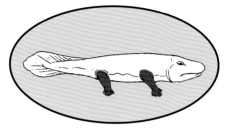

STEP 2   Some with jaws have four limbs with digits.

STEP 3   Some with four limbs and digits produce special eggs that resist drying out.

STEP 4   Some with special eggs have a characteristic skull opening.

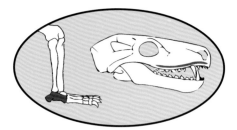

STEP 5   Some with the skull opening have heels on their feet and a palate separating the nasal passage from the mouth.

STEP 6   Finally, a small number with heels and a palate have a unique set of traits: hair, the females' ability to suckle their young, three bones in the middle ear, and a mouth equipped with different kinds of teeth for different jobs. This last group is mammals!

Now go backward, and you'll be seeing the evolutionary history of mammals!

The Day of the Dinosaur Has Begun

It's 230 million years ago, late in the Triassic Period. A new predator has been terrorizing the land. It stands on two legs, it can run, and it can take down its prey with razor-sharp claws and teeth like knives.

It's one of the first dinosaurs. It isn't that much bigger than some of the other reptiles around. But just wait and see what happens over the next 160 million years.

With a length of ten feet, *Herrerasaurus* is small compared to *T. rex* and other meat-eating dinosaurs that will come later, but you don't want to get in its way. It's one of the fiercest predators of its day.

What Is a Dinosaur?

Dinosaurs belong to a group of reptiles that has been around for a while: diapsid reptiles. Diapsid reptiles have a unique type of skull that has two openings behind each eye socket. *Youngina* was a Permian diapsid reptile. *Angistorhinus* and *Isalorhynchus* are Triassic diapsid reptiles. (All modern-day reptiles—such as lizards, snakes, crocodiles, and turtles—are diapsid reptiles.)

THESE REPTILES ARE NOT DINOSAURS

◀ *Youngina*

▶ *Angistorhinus*

◀ *Isalorhynchus*

But dinosaurs have something that makes them unique among all reptiles.

Look at the way most reptiles stand. Their legs sprawl sideways from their bodies.

Now look at the way dinosaurs stand. Their legs extend straight down underneath their bodies. This may be what allowed dinosaurs to grow so large: A skeleton put together this way can support more weight.

THESE REPTILES ARE DINOSAURS

▲ *Parasaurolophus*

◄ *Brachiosaurus*

► *Daspletosaurus*

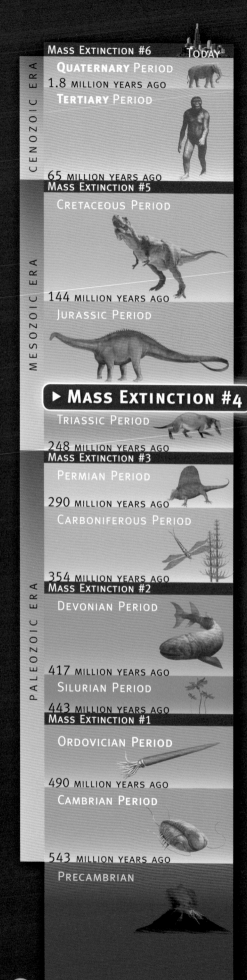

MASS EXTINCTION #4

It's the end of the Triassic Period, and dinosaurs are just about to have their day on Earth. The planet is a great place for dinosaurs right now. But for the last nineteen million years or so, many other species have been suffering. Scores of marine animals, land plants, and tetrapods have gone extinct.

This mass extinction is nowhere near as devastating as the last one, which wiped out nine out of every ten species. But the reasons for extinction may have been similar: climate change. The Triassic Period was a very warm time, and global warming at the end of the Triassic made it even warmer. Species not adapted to these soaring temperatures would have suffered. Close to half of marine animal species have gone extinct. Land plants are hard hit too: In some parts of the world, as many as 95 percent of plant species are now gone. And when plants start dying out, the animals that eat them are in trouble.

◀ The fourth mass extinction happened at the end of the Triassic Period, from around 225 million to 206 million years ago.

Meet the Armored Dinosaurs: The Thyreophorans

Spiky tails and spiky shoulders. Rows of plates the size of sharks' fins. Now we're in the Jurassic and Cretaceous periods, and these lumpy-looking dinosaurs are everywhere. They are called thyreophorans, and they have bony plates, called osteoderms, on their bodies.

They may look threatening, but thyreophorans are plant eaters. Since they aren't predators, all that armor is their best protection. And it must be pretty good protection: thyreophorans are spectacular sights on the Mesozoic scene for more than 130 million years.

◀ *Stegosaurus*
LENGTH: *20 feet*
LIVED: *150 million years ago*

You can't miss *Stegosaurus,* with those rows of osteoderms along its back. What are they for? Maybe they attract mates or scare off rivals. And stay out of the way of that spiky tail. If *Stegosaurus* feels threatened, that tail can be a fearsome weapon.

▶ *Edmontonia*
LENGTH: *20 feet*
LIVED: *70 million years ago*

Edmontonia is an ankylosaur. Built for self-defense, ankylosaurs are the "tanks" of the Mesozoic Era. A predator trying to make a meal of *Edmontonia* could get a spike in the mouth or break a tooth on that shield of bony osteoderms.

Meet the Largest Creatures Ever to Walk the Earth: The Sauropods

You can't miss the sauropods. They are enormous. Nothing this large has ever lived on land before. The largest can grow to more than a hundred feet long (that's longer than two school buses!) and weigh as much as seventy tons (that's heavier than ten elephants!).

These long-necked, long-legged, all-around-long plant eaters are a major Mesozoic success story. Their size is their advantage. Even the most fearsome predators have a hard time preying on them, and they can reach high treetops that smaller plant eaters can't reach.

◀ *Brachiosaurus*
LENGTH: *70 feet*
LIVED: *150 million years ago*

The forty-foot-tall *Brachiosaurus* can feed from the very highest treetops of the Jurassic. Its front legs are longer than its hind legs, giving it extra height and an extra boost to reach places even other sauropods can't.

◀ *Apatosaurus*
LENGTH: *72 feet*
LIVED: *150 million years ago*

The tail on *Apatosaurus* makes up more than half this gigantic dinosaur's length. There are around eighty bones in its tail alone. (In your entire backbone, you have only thirty-three!) *Apatosaurus* might lash that impressive tail like a whip when a predator threatens.

▶ *Lufengosaurus*
LENGTH: *20 feet*
LIVED: *200 million years ago*

Prosauropods are a very early crew of dinosaurs that are related to sauropods—but smaller. The first ones evolved back in the Triassic, but they are still around in the Jurassic. This one is *Lufengosaurus*. Like other prosauropods, *Lufengosaurus* has an interesting skill: When it wants to, it can stand up and move on two legs. No big, lumbering sauropod can do that!

◀ *Rapetosaurus*
LENGTH: *50 feet*
LIVED: *70 million years ago*

After all the other sauropods die out, *Rapetosaurus* and the other titanosaurs remain. Titanosaurs have a much wider stance than other sauropods, with their broad chests and wide hips. And many have bony armor in their skin to help protect them against a predator's lethal bite.

Meet the Meat Eaters: The Theropods

Here they are, the killers of the dinosaur world. These are the most fearsome predators of the Mesozoic: the theropods. *Tyrannosaurus rex* (*T. rex*) is just one of many. They are the only carnivorous (meat-eating) dinosaurs in a world of plant eaters.

Tyrannosaurus rex. One of the largest known predators of all time, this Cretaceous killer has few rivals. It can't run very fast, and its tiny forelimbs aren't good for much. But its skull is massive, its teeth are the size of hunting knives, and its jaws are powerful enough to break bone.

T. rex also has an excellent sense of smell. If this predator gets a whiff of you and catches you by surprise, you don't stand a chance. Like a lot of hunters, *T. rex* would eat dead animals if it found them, but *T. rex* was—first and foremost—a killing machine.

But there's something else that sets theropods apart. They are the only dinosaurs that won't go extinct: Birds are theropods! That's right; when you get back home and look at the modern-day birds around you, you'll be looking at real, live dinosaurs.

▼ *Tyrannosaurus rex*
LENGTH: *42 feet*
LIVED: *67 million years ago*

Theropods like *Allosaurus* and *Cryolophosaurus* can have some pretty crazy headgear, with horns, knobs, and bumpy crests adorning their skulls. These fancy ornaments are probably for show, scaring off rivals—or maybe making a male dinosaur look good to a mate!

▶ **Allosaurus**
LENGTH: *35 feet*
LIVED: *150 million years ago*

◀ **Daspletosaurus**
LENGTH: *30 feet*
LIVED: *75 million years ago*

Daspletosaurus and *Majungasaurus* might not be quite the size of *T. rex,* but they're still a lot bigger than you. Wherever you go in the Mesozoic world, there are big theropod predators looking for their next meal.

▶ **Majungasaurus**
LENGTH: *30 feet*
LIVED: *70 million years ago*

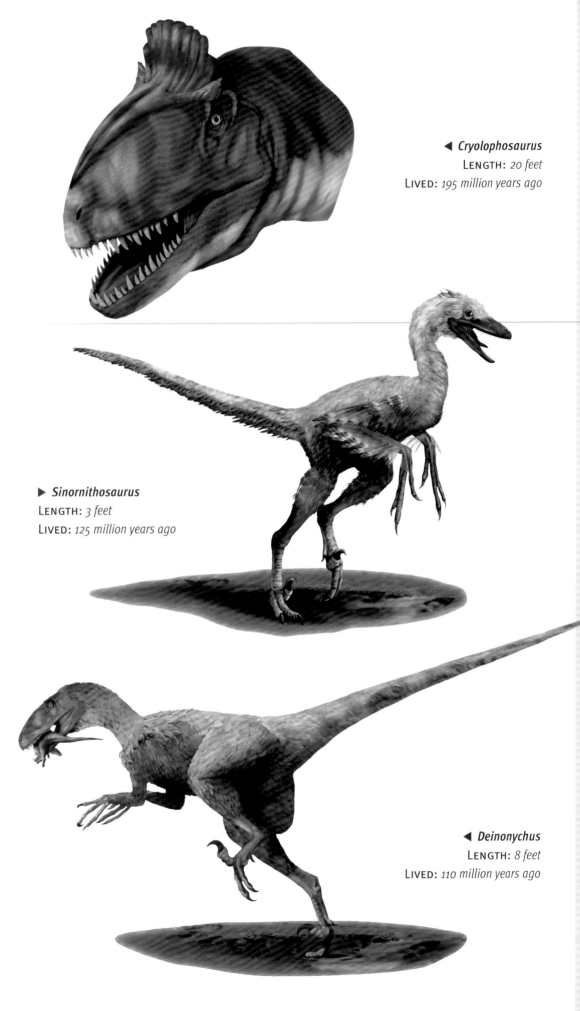

◀ *Cryolophosaurus*
LENGTH: *20 feet*
LIVED: *195 million years ago*

▶ *Sinornithosaurus*
LENGTH: *3 feet*
LIVED: *125 million years ago*

◀ *Deinonychus*
LENGTH: *8 feet*
LIVED: *110 million years ago*

A well-placed kick from *Sinornithosaurus* or *Deinonychus* will mean certain death for their unlucky prey. These theropods are the "raptors." The sickle-shaped claws on their middle toes can slash like a lethal blade. And are those—feathers? That's right, theropods include some very familiar animals: birds. "Raptors" aren't birds—just some of birds' closest dinosaur relatives. They can't fly, but there are reasons why some theropods might have evolved feathers. Maybe they help keep these dinosaurs warm. Or maybe feathers give some extra lift when a theropod makes a leap for fast-moving prey, helping them to make the kill.

Some theropods can fly! That's right, birds are theropod dinosaurs, and *Archaeopteryx* (below center) is an early bird. Birds have one key thing setting them apart from the "raptors," their closest dinosaur relatives: Their front limbs are longer than their hind limbs. It's easy to see how, with feathers, these long "arms" have evolved into wings!

▲ Flying reptiles, primitive birds, and two tiny dinosaurs

Meet the Ornithopods: The "Duck-Bills" & Their Close Relatives

These dinosaurs are everywhere you look. They are the largest and most diverse dinosaur group: the ornithopods. These plant eaters are the "cows of the Cretaceous," and like cows, they have cheeks, which means they can hold their food in their mouths while they chew.

Many of them have mouths that look like a duck's bill. Some have elaborate, bony crests on their heads. They are bipedal—they walk on two legs—but often, they get down on all fours to munch on low-growing leaves or to take a drink at a watering hole. Ornithopods dominate the Mesozoic landscape, moving in herds, constantly grazing, pausing now and then to be on the lookout for predators.

◀ *Parasaurolophus*
LENGTH: *30 feet*
LIVED: *75 million years ago*

If we stick around, we might hear *Parasaurolophus* use that bony head crest like a trumpet! The crest is hollow and by blowing air through it, *Parasaurolophus* might communicate with its fellow species using a symphony of sounds. Imagine a whole herd in full cry!

▶ *Lambeosaurus*
LENGTH: *30 feet*
LIVED: *75 million years ago*

Lambeosaurus has fallen prey to a hungry *Daspletosaurus*. An ornithopod herd can outrun a big, slow theropod—unless it gets taken by surprise. Then, an unlucky member of the herd might become dinner for a hunter on the attack.

Meet the Marginocephalians, with Their Bony Frills

These dinosaurs have some eye-catching headgear. They are the marginocephalians, and they all share something special: a "frill" of bone at the back of the skull. Sometimes it's a big frill; sometimes it's small. Sometimes it comes with horns, or a thick bony dome. But it's always there, sticking out over the back of the dinosaur's neck like the rim of a football helmet.

These dinosaurs may look mean, but they are plant eaters, not predators. Their sharp-looking beaks are for snipping leafy bites, not for going on the attack. All those bones and domes and spikes are just for show! They make these dinosaurs look bigger and help them impress potential mates.

Earlier in the Cretaceous, little *Protoceratops* is a typical marginocephalian dinosaur. It's pretty small—about the size of a large dog—and it doesn't have the fancy frill some of its larger, later cousins will have.

▲ *Protoceratops*
LENGTH: *5 feet*
LIVED: *80 million years ago*

◀ Triceratops
LENGTH: *30 feet*
LIVED: *67 million years ago*

Frills don't get fancier than the ones on *Triceratops* and *Anchiceratops,* who live later on in the Cretaceous. As time goes on and marginocephalians get bigger, their frills get bigger. Horns on their faces make these dinosaurs look even more impressive! Who are they trying to impress? One another, probably—either rivals or potential mates.

▶ Anchiceratops
LENGTH: *20 feet*
LIVED: *70 million years ago*

◀ Stegoceras
LENGTH: *6 feet*
LIVED: *70 million years ago*

Stegoceras may have just a tiny frill, but its skull sports a four-inch-thick dome of bone. What's it for? Maybe that telltale bony head helps one *Stegoceras* recognize another.

Flowers Bloom

Plants provide shade, shelter, and supper for many types of animals, from the tiniest insects to the tallest dinosaurs. Ferns, cycads, conifers, and ginkgos are common in the Triassic and Jurassic periods. Early in the Cretaceous Period, something new has joined them—flowers! Plants with flowers, called angiosperms, protect their seeds inside a fruit. Can you think of any modern-day fruits? Apples, peaches, and peanuts are just a few!

Archaeanthus is one of the very first plants with flowers. It looks much like the modern-day magnolia. The cone-shaped structures of *Archaeanthus* become the plant's fruit.

An Age of Reptiles

With the likes of mighty *Apatosaurus* and ferocious *Tyrannosaurus*, reptiles rule the Mesozoic Era. But dinosaurs are only part of the picture. Up in the skies, flying reptiles called pterosaurs soar. And look down. Crocodiles, turtles, lizards, and snakes have all evolved! Many look like their cousins back in the modern world, but some are quite unlike anything you've ever seen.

The first crocodiles, like *Dibothrosuchus*, can run fast. No modern-day croc has such long legs!

▲ *Dibothrosuchus*
LENGTH: *3 feet*
LIVED: *205 million years ago*

Steneosaurus uses its powerful tail and large, paddle-like feet to swim the seas. It may look like modern-day crocodiles, but no modern crocs swim the deep seas.

▲ *Steneosaurus*
LENGTH: *10 feet*
LIVED: *160 million years ago*

▲ *Mahajangasuchus*
LENGTH: *13 feet*
LIVED: *70 million years ago*

With its massive jaws
and pointy teeth,
Mahajangasuchus is a vicious
meat eater. But pug-nosed
Simosuchus is a peaceful plant
eater. It has teeth shaped like
little leaves, good for cutting
up plants. Crocodiles of the
Mesozoic have all kinds of
diets.

◀ *Simosuchus*
LENGTH: *3 feet*
LIVED: *70 million years ago*

Unlike the crocodiles, turtles
such as *Toxochelys* look like
modern-day ones. With tough
shells that provide good
protection from predators, why
change?

▲ *Toxochelys*
LENGTH: *3.5 feet*
LIVED: *85 million years ago*

Rhamphorhynchus and *Nyctosaurus* are pterosaurs—reptiles that took to the skies! Pterosaurs are not dinosaurs. And since pterosaurs are not dinosaurs, they also cannot be birds—because birds *are* dinosaurs. Instead, pterosaurs are a unique type of reptile that first evolved during the Triassic Period. Unlike birds, which have feathers, pterosaurs have wings made from skin that's attached to their arms and to one long finger on each hand. Some pterosaurs are the size of a blue jay. Others—with a wingspan of forty feet—are the largest animals ever to fly.

Its sharp teeth help *Rhamphorhynchus* catch insects and other prey. To chase them, it uses its long rudder-like tail to maneuver and steer through the air.

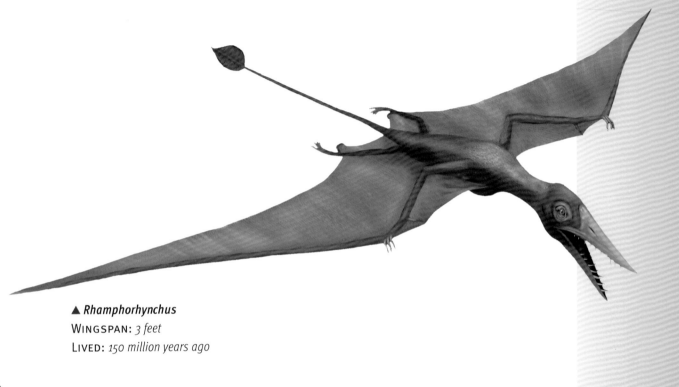

▲ *Rhamphorhynchus*
WINGSPAN: *3 feet*
LIVED: *150 million years ago*

◀ *Nyctosaurus*
WINGSPAN: *9 feet*
LIVED: *85 million years ago*

With its long, toothless beak, *Nyctosaurus* hunts over the shallow seas, swooping down to grab a tasty fish!

Dive into the Mesozoic Seas

The mass extinction at the end of the Permian Period wiped out 90 percent of life in the seas. Let's take an underwater journey through the Mesozoic seas and see how life recovered. Things may seem familiar at first. But be careful! There are fearsome reptiles in these waters that you won't see in any modern-day seas.

Corals such as *Guembelastraea*, sea urchins such as *Plegiocidaris*, and snails such as *Pleurotomaria* look very similar to their modern-day cousins. Crabs and lobsters also live in these seas!

◄ *Guembelastraea*
WIDTH: *3 inches*
LIVED: *220 million years ago*

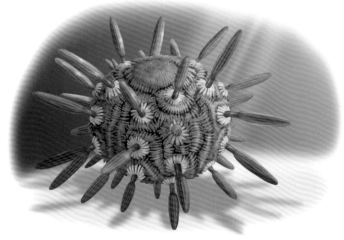

► *Plegiocidaris*
WIDTH: *2.5 inches*
LIVED: *150 million years ago*

◄ *Pleurotomaria*
LENGTH: *3 inches*
LIVED: *170 million years ago*

◀ **Belemnitella**
LENGTH: *16 inches*
LIVED: *72 million years ago*

Belemnitella and *Mortoniceras* are mollusks. They are closely related to modern-day squids and octopi, and they both use their muscular tentacles for grasping food or moving around.

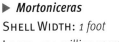 **Mortoniceras**
SHELL WIDTH: *1 foot*
LIVED: *100 million years ago*

Belemnitella is a special type of mollusk called a belemnite. *Mortoniceras* is another type called an ammonoid. Both belemnites and ammonoids are very common in the seas of the Mesozoic Era.

◀ **Pholidophorus**
LENGTH: *7 inches*
LIVED: *200 million years ago*

Remember *Palaeoniscum* from way back in the Paleozoic Era? Fishes like *Pholidophorus* and the giant *Xiphactinus* are similar types of fishes. All have fins made of fine bones surrounded by a thin web of skin. Back in the modern world, more of these types of fishes swim the planet's lakes, rivers, seas, and oceans than any other type of fish.

 Xiphactinus
LENGTH: *20 feet*
LIVED: *85 million years ago*

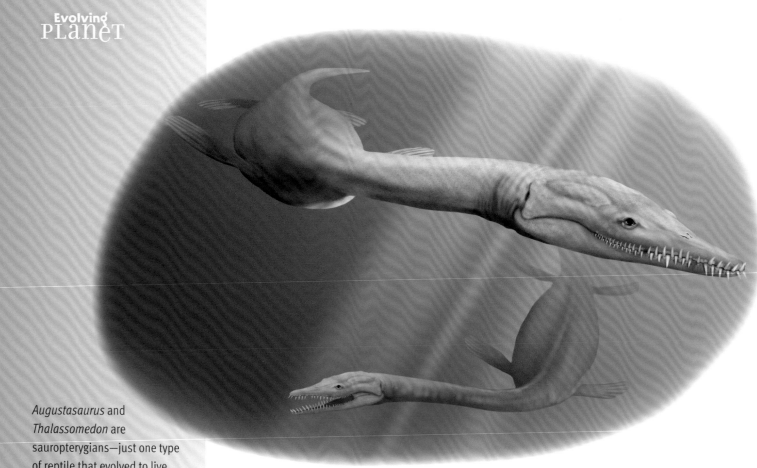

Augustasaurus and
Thalassomedon are
sauropterygians—just one type
of reptile that evolved to live
in the seas. Augustasaurus
chases its prey with its
webbed hands and feet.
Thalassomedon has broad
paddles that it moves up and
down the way a bird moves its
wings. Its long neck can coil
and surprise its prey with a
lightning-quick strike!

▲ *Augustasaurus*
LENGTH: *10 feet*
LIVED: *235 million years ago*

▲ *Thalassomedon*
LENGTH: *40 feet*
LIVED: *95 million years ago*

Although it looks like a dolphin or shark, *Stenopterygius* is actually a type of reptile called an ichthyosaur. With its fish-like body and enormous eyes, *Stenopterygius* is well adapted for cruising the open oceans and exploring its darkest depths.

▲ *Stenopterygius*
LENGTH: *4 feet*
LIVED: *185 million years ago*

With a long, powerful tail to propel it through the water, fin-shaped limbs for agile steering, and a mouth full of sharp teeth, *Platecarpus* is a perfect killer. *Platecarpus* belongs to the group of swimming reptiles called mosasaurs. Mosasaurs are lizards that evolved to live in the seas. They are closely related to the Komodo dragon back in the modern world.

▲ *Platecarpus*
LENGTH: *20 feet*
LIVED: *85 million years ago*

MASS EXTINCTION #6
QUATERNARY PERIOD
TODAY
1.8 MILLION YEARS AGO
TERTIARY PERIOD

CENOZOIC ERA

▶ **MASS EXTINCTION #5**

CRETACEOUS PERIOD

MESOZOIC ERA

144 MILLION YEARS AGO
JURASSIC PERIOD

206 MILLION YEARS AGO
MASS EXTINCTION #4
TRIASSIC PERIOD

248 MILLION YEARS AGO
MASS EXTINCTION #3
PERMIAN PERIOD

290 MILLION YEARS AGO
CARBONIFEROUS PERIOD

PALEOZOIC ERA

354 MILLION YEARS AGO
MASS EXTINCTION #2
DEVONIAN PERIOD

417 MILLION YEARS AGO
SILURIAN PERIOD

443 MILLION YEARS AGO
MASS EXTINCTION #1

ORDOVICIAN PERIOD

490 MILLION YEARS AGO
CAMBRIAN PERIOD

543 MILLION YEARS AGO
PRECAMBRIAN

◀ The fifth mass extinction happened sixty-five million years ago.

80

4.5 BILLION YEARS AGO

MASS EXTINCTION #5

It's sixty-five million years ago, the end of the Cretaceous Period. Dinosaurs have ruled the earth for the last 160 million years. Now they are nowhere to be seen.

Mass extinction has struck the planet yet again. Half of all life on Earth has been wiped out. The giant marine reptiles that swam the seas are gone. So are the pterosaurs, those magnificent winged reptiles in the skies.

And all dinosaurs—except for the birds—are gone.

What happened? What catastrophe could have ended the age of dinosaurs?

It probably was several things at once making the planet a tough place to live. For one thing, a gigantic meteorite collided with Earth. When this happened, massive quantities of dust and other particles filled the atmosphere around the globe. These particles probably changed the climate in some way. They might have blocked the sun's rays, cooling things down. Or they might have trapped heat and gases close to Earth's surface, warming things up. Either way, this could have spelled doom for much life on the planet; when the climate changes too much, it can be hard for many species to survive.

But there is more. Some very large volcanoes have been erupting almost nonstop for a few million years, pouring out lava and gases. These gases could also have trapped heat close to Earth's surface. It's another thing that could have caused the climate to change—and when the climate changes, life can suffer.

The Geologic Time Scale

CENOZOIC ERA

TODAY

QUATERNARY PERIOD
1.8 MILLION YEARS AGO
TERTIARY PERIOD

You are here

MESOZOIC ERA

CRETACEOUS PERIOD

144 MILLION YEARS AGO
JURASSIC PERIOD

206 MILLION YEARS AGO
TRIASSIC PERIOD

248 MILLION YEARS AGO
PERMIAN PERIOD

PALEOZOIC ERA

290 MILLION YEARS AGO
CARBONIFEROUS PERIOD

354 MILLION YEARS AGO
DEVONIAN PERIOD

417 MILLION YEARS AGO
SILURIAN PERIOD

443 MILLION YEARS AGO
ORDOVICIAN PERIOD

490 MILLION YEARS AGO
CAMBRIAN PERIOD

543 MILLION YEARS AGO
PRECAMBRIAN

◀ You are here: The Tertiary Period.

▼ The continents have almost arrived at their modern-day positions. It is very warm, and there are no ice caps at the poles.

65 MILLION YEARS AGO

Mammals Inherit the Earth

THE TERTIARY PERIOD
65–1.8 million years ago

It's a new day. The sun shines bright and animals stir. High in the trees, early relatives of primates scurry about, keeping a watchful eye as they search for a midday snack. Two lumbering, bear-like pantodonts pass through a clearing below. And small horses, no bigger than dogs, frolic about. It is a new world. It is a world of mammals.

At the end of the Cretaceous Period, mass extinction devastated life on Earth. Gone are the flying pterosaurs, the ferocious swimming reptiles, and all dinosaurs except birds. Crocodiles, lizards, and other reptiles survived, but reptiles will never again rule the land as did the dinosaurs. The age of reptiles is over.

The world now belongs to those that survived the extinction. On land, the spaces left empty by the dinosaurs are being filled—by mammals. For the rest of our journey, we'll watch the mammals. You will see horses and camels, cats and dogs, and other familiar forms arrive on the scene, and you'll see a certain group of apes evolve into humans.

Tertiary Period, fifty-five million years ago

A New Age Begins with New Mammals

For 150 million years, mammals lived in the shadows of the mighty dinosaurs. Most were shrew-like and no bigger than a shoe.

But the beginning of the Tertiary Period is a much different world. There are no big dinosaurs. It's safer, and there's less competition for food. In this new world, new types of mammals evolve. Let's meet some of them. And keep in mind the mammals back in the modern world— particularly cats, dogs, horses, and apes. You'll see the beginnings of their family trees.

Puppy-size *Hyracotherium* is the very first horse! But unlike modern-day horses, which have one hoof on each foot, it has four hooves on each of its front feet and three on each of its hind feet. Hooves provide a stable platform for walking, running, and standing. And as we continue our journey, you'll see that many different types of mammals have hooves. *Hyracotherium* is one of the first.

▶ *Hyracotherium*
LENGTH: *2 feet*
LIVED: *55 million years ago*

▼ *Didymictis*
LENGTH: *3 feet*
LIVED: *55 million years ago*

Didymictis is a special type of mammal called a carnivoran. Carnivorans eat meat, and they have scissor-like teeth to help slice it! Cats, dogs, bears, seals, raccoons, weasels—all are modern-day carnivorans.

◀ *Paramys*
LENGTH: *1 foot*
LIVED: *55 million years ago*

Paramys is one of the first rodents. And like all rodents, it has large incisors—the teeth at the front of the mouth—that never stop growing, good for gnawing.

Climbing up in the trees is lemur-like *Notharctus*. With its grasping hands and feet, forward-facing eyes, and large brain, this early primate has much in common with its modern-day relatives. And that includes you!

▶ *Notharctus*
LENGTH: *2 feet*
LIVED: *50 million years ago*

◄ *Barylambda*
LENGTH: *7 feet*
LIVED: *55 million years ago*

Not all mammals in this new world have modern-day descendants. *Barylambda* and *Coryphodon* are pantodonts—large, lumbering plant eaters that will soon go extinct. And it may look like a rhinoceros, but *Eobasileus* is not closely related to the rhino. It's a uintathere, another soon-to-be-extinct type of mammal.

▲ *Coryphodon*
LENGTH: *10 feet*
LIVED: *55 million years ago*

◄ *Eobasileus*
LENGTH: *10 feet*
LIVED: *45 million years ago*

A Tropical Planet

The world after the dinosaurs is very warm. How warm? Let's look at the place we call Wyoming today. During the Tertiary Period, massive lakes are home to crocodiles, turtles, and fishes. Palm trees and other plants make up lush tropical forests. Birds and insects fly through the air; mammals and lizards climb, scurry, or swim. Back in the modern world, this area is very different: a rocky, high mountain desert with long, cold, snowy winters. The planet is always changing, and so is its climate!

▲ Wyoming during the Tertiary Period

◀ Wyoming today, fifty million years later

Trapped in Stone

A FABULOUS FOSSIL SITE:
Fossil Lake, Wyoming, USA

As we journey through time, we are seeing some amazing plants and animals. Five-eyed *Opabinia* from the Cambrian, the great forests of the Carboniferous, and the truly titanic *Brachiosaurus* from the Jurassic.

After these organisms die, they sometimes become fossils. Let's travel ahead to our own time and look at the wonderful fifty-million-year-old fossils that scientists have found at Fossil Lake, Wyoming. These fossils paint a picture of ancient tropical forests and lakes.

These fossilized leaves are from plants that thrive in warm, wet environments. They're clues to Wyoming's lush past.

▶ Palm frond (*Sabalites*)
HEIGHT: *6 feet*
LIVED: *50 million years ago*

◀ Leaf from a close relative of the cacao tree (*Sterculia*)
LENGTH: *4 inches*
LIVED: *50 million years ago*

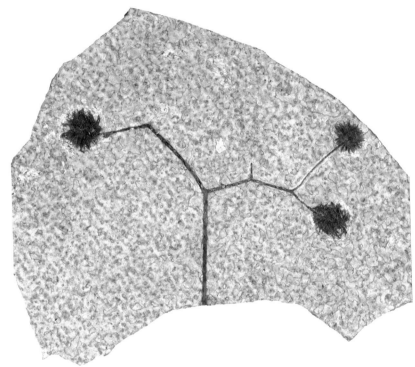

◀ Branch with fruit from a sycamore tree (*Platanus*)
WIDTH: *5 inches*
LIVED: *50 million years ago*

▼ Cattail (*Typha*)
LENGTH: *10 inches*
LIVED: *50 million years ago*

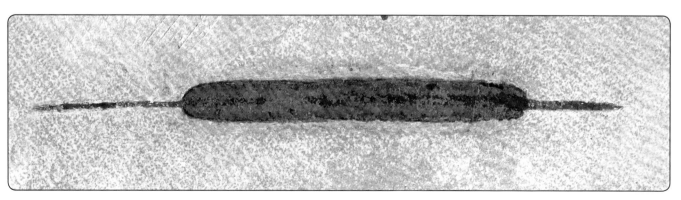

▶ Leaf from a close relative of
the soapberry tree (*Allophylus*)
LENGTH: *5 inches*
LIVED: *50 million years ago*

▶ Fern frond (*Cladophlebis*)
LENGTH: *5 inches*
LIVED: *50 million years ago*

▶ Among the fossils from
Wyoming's ancient lakes are
some of the oldest known
complete bat skeletons
(*Icaronycteris*).
LENGTH: *4 inches*
LIVED: *50 million years ago*

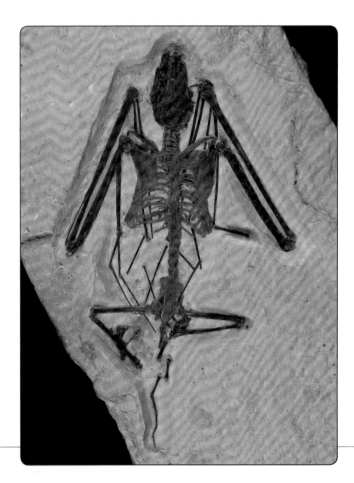

◄ In the trees, the carnivoran mammal *Paroodectes* hunted its prey.
LENGTH: *2.5 feet*
LIVED: *50 million years ago*

The lizard *Saniwa* (right) may have been a fierce meat eater, but the crocodile *Leidyosuchus* (below) ruled the ancient Wyoming lakes.

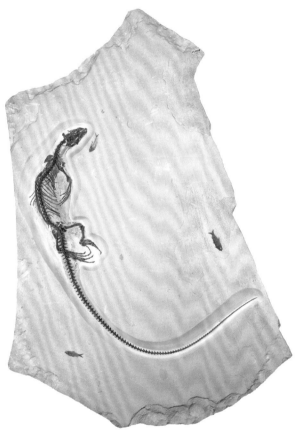

◄ *Saniwa*
LENGTH: *4 feet*
LIVED: *50 million years ago*

▼ *Leidyosuchus*
LENGTH: *12 feet*
LIVED: *50 million years ago*

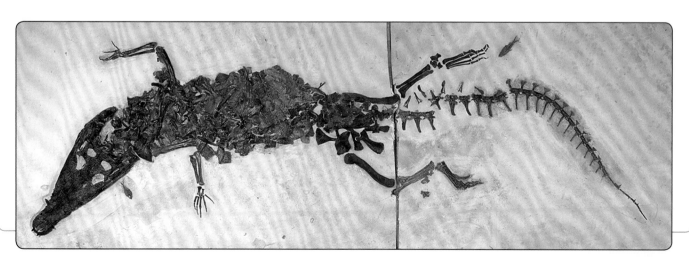

Flying high above the lakes and forests were birds like this one. Even fossils of feathers are preserved!

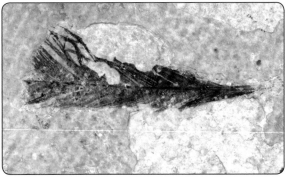

▲ **LENGTH:** *1.5 inches*
LIVED: *50 million years ago*

▶ **HEIGHT:** *5 inches*
LIVED: *50 million years ago*

In addition to fishes, turtles and frogs lived in Wyoming's tropical lakes.

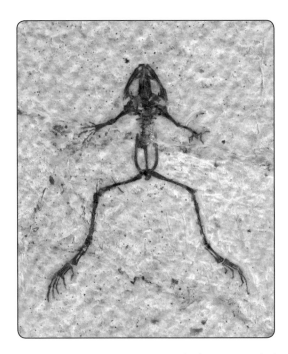

▲ **LENGTH:** *1.5 inches*
LIVED: *50 million years ago*

▶ **LENGTH:** *14 inches*
LIVED: *50 million years ago*

Fossils from Wyoming's lakes even show tiny ants, spiders, and the delicate wings of dragonflies.

▲ LENGTH: *0.1 inches*
LIVED: *50 million years ago*

▶ LENGTH: *0.5 inches*
LIVED: *50 million years ago*

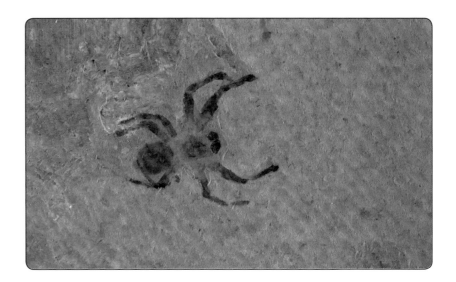

◀ WINGSPAN: *2.5 inches*
LIVED: *50 million years ago*

Many different types of fishes swam the lakes of ancient Wyoming.

▶ Gar (*Atractosteus*)
LENGTH: *2 feet*
LIVED: *50 million years ago*

▶ Bonytongue fish
(*Phareodus*)
LENGTH: 2 feet
LIVED: *50 million years ago*

▶ Spiny-finned fish
(*Priscacara*)
LENGTH: *3.5 inches*
LIVED: *50 million years ago*

◀ Pickerel (*Esox*)
Length: *4.5 inches*
Lived: *50 million years ago*

Stingray (*Asterotrygon*) and fish (*Priscacara*)
▼ **Length:** *6 inches*
Lived: *50 million years ago*

▲ **Length:** *14 inches*
Lived: *50 million years ago*

► Bowfin (*Amia*)
LENGTH: *3.5 feet*
LIVED: *50 million years ago*

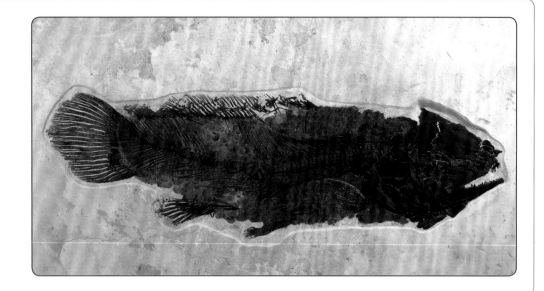

Some fossils not only show the fish, but its dinner, too!

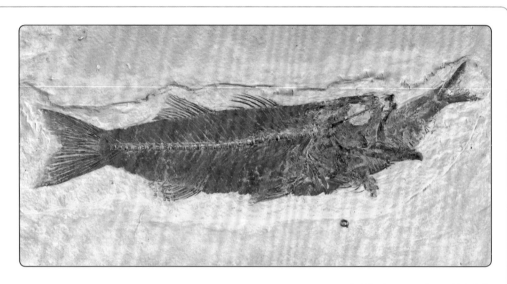

▼ A paddlefish (*Crossopholis*) with other fishes in its stomach
LENGTH: *2.5 feet*
LIVED: *50 million years ago*

▲ A *Mioplosus* eating a *Knightia*
LENGTH: *6.5 inches*
LIVED: *50 million years ago*

So many fossils! Scientists find fossils of fishes of all ages—from young to old—so they can even see how a fish like *Priscacara* grew during its lifetime.

▲ **LENGTH:** *0.5 inches*
LIVED: *50 million years ago*

▲ **LENGTH:** *1 inch*
LIVED: *50 million years ago*

▲ **LENGTH:** *1.5 inches*
LIVED: *50 million years ago*

▲ **LENGTH:** *4.5 inches*
LIVED: *50 million years ago*

▲ **LENGTH:** *6.5 inches*
LIVED: *50 million years ago*

◄ **LENGTH:** *1 foot*
LIVED: *50 million years ago*

Grasslands of North America

We are now back in the Tertiary Period. But something is different. Temperatures around the planet have cooled. The lush tropical forests—such as the one we saw in ancient Wyoming—are mostly gone. You can only find them near the equator now.

What covers the rest of the world? Grasses! Grasses are well adapted for cool, dry climates. So cooling temperatures led to the spread of vast grasslands. And as grasses grow, the mammals that eat them (and the mammals that eat those mammals) continue to evolve.

Horse history is a story of *many* different species. Over time, we can see horses change as grasslands spread. It all started with little *Hyracotherium*, which had many small toes for maneuvering through forests. Like all horses, each toe ended with a hoof. *Mesohippus* has longer legs and a bigger central toe and hoof, good for running across open grasslands. And *Pliohippus* will have even longer legs and an even bigger toe and hoof.

◀ *Hyracotherium*
LENGTH: *2 feet*
LIVED: *55 million years ago*

▶ *Mesohippus*
LENGTH: *3 feet*
LIVED: *35 million years ago*

▶ Pliohippus
LENGTH: *6 feet*
LIVED: *15 million years ago*

◀ Trigonias
LENGTH: *8 feet*
LIVED: *35 million years ago*

Rhinoceroses have evolved! Early rhinos like *Trigonias* feed on the leaves of trees and shrubs. But stubby *Teleoceras* enjoys the newly abundant grasses.

▶ Teleoceras
LENGTH: *8 feet*
LIVED: *10 million years ago*

Titanotheres like *Menodus* are some of the largest mammals around. But unlike other plant-eating hoofed mammals, such as horses and rhinos, they will soon go extinct.

▶ *Menodus*
LENGTH: *9 feet*
LIVED: *35 million years ago*

◀ *Moropus*
LENGTH: *8 feet*
LIVED: *20 million years ago*

Not all mammals are eating grasses: *Moropus* and *Oxydactylus* use their long legs and necks to reach tasty leaves. *Oxydactylus* is a camel. *Moropus* is a chalicothere. Chalicotheres have longer front legs than back legs—good for reaching high branches—and their large front claws are good for reaching up to bring down a leafy bite. Camels will survive, but chalicotheres will eventually go extinct.

▶ *Oxydactylus*
LENGTH: *7 feet*
LIVED: *20 million years ago*

It may look different from its modern-day cousins, but *Gomphotherium* is an elephant. Instead of just two tusks, *Gomphotherium* has four—two on top and two on the bottom.

◀ *Gomphotherium*
LENGTH: *12 feet*
LIVED: *10 million years ago*

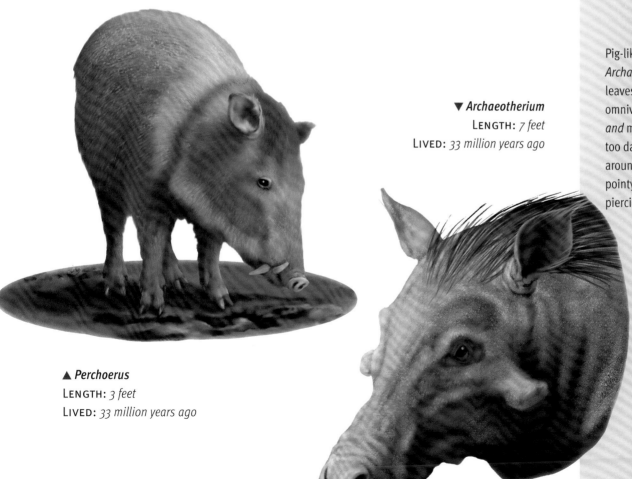

▼ *Archaeotherium*
LENGTH: *7 feet*
LIVED: *33 million years ago*

Pig-like *Perchoerus* and *Archaeotherium* don't eat just leaves or grasses. They are omnivores; they eat plants *and* meat. *Perchoerus* is not too dangerous, but be careful around *Archaeotherium*—its pointy teeth are good for piercing and cutting flesh!

▲ *Perchoerus*
LENGTH: *3 feet*
LIVED: *33 million years ago*

What's new, pussycat? You! And dogs, too! It's among the new grass-eating mammals that cats and dogs evolved. *Dinictis* is one of the first cats, and little *Hesperocyon* is one of the first dogs.

▲ *Dinictis*
LENGTH: *4 feet*
LIVED: *33 million years ago*

▶ *Hesperocyon*
LENGTH: *3 feet*
LIVED: *33 million years ago*

The Grasslands of South America

In South America, mammals are thriving. But there are no horses, cats, or dogs, as there are in North America. The land masses that today form these two continents are not attached. They are each one big island, and on each, different types of mammals evolve.

Its long front claws may look vicious, but bulky *Homalodotherium* is a gentle giant. Its claws help pull down tree branches for a leafy bite.

▶ *Homalodotherium*
LENGTH: *6 feet*
LIVED: *15 million years ago*

◀ *Craumauchenia*
LENGTH: *6 feet*
LIVED: *25 million years ago*

Although *Craumauchenia* looks like a camel, it is not. But like camels in North America, *Craumauchenia* does use its long neck to feed high in the trees.

▶ *Andalgalornis*
HEIGHT: *5 feet*
LIVED: *5 million years ago*

Able to run nearly forty miles per hour and equipped with a sharp, powerful beak, birds like *Andalgalornis* are fierce meat eaters. In most of the world, carnivoran mammals (a special group of mammals that have scissor-like teeth) such as cats and dogs are the top predators. With no carnivorans in South America, birds rule.

◀ *Thylacosmilus*
LENGTH: *6 feet*
LIVED: *5 million years ago*

Thylacosmilus uses its sharp saber teeth to kill its prey. And although it may look like a cat, *Thylacosmilus* is a marsupial, not a carnivoran. It's closely related to modern-day koalas and kangaroos!

EVOLUTION
How It Works & How We Know
CONVERGENT EVOLUTION

In the Tertiary Period, the cat-like carnivoran *Hoplophoneus* hunts across North America with its fearsome saber teeth. In South America, the marsupial *Thylacosmilus* also has sharp saber teeth.

Having evolved on completely different land masses, how did two only distantly related species wind up with such similar saber teeth?

When different species are faced with similar environmental challenges, natural selection sometimes favors similar features. It's called convergent evolution.

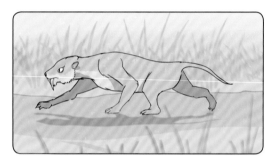

Both *Hoplophoneus* (left) and *Thylacosmilus* (right) are hunters. And long saber teeth are good for killing prey, so both happened to evolve the same tool for the job. It's that easy!

Other examples of convergent evolution? You may have noticed that the dinosaur *Brachiosaurus* has a long neck and longer front legs than back legs, like a giraffe. That's because both *Brachiosaurus* and a giraffe feed high in the treetops. And ichthyosaurs—those swimming reptiles from the Mesozoic Era—look a lot like dolphins, which are swimming mammals.

That's convergent evolution. If something worked once, it might turn up again!

New Primates Evolve: Apes

There's a rustling of branches overhead. A shrill cry shatters the quiet of a hot jungle afternoon. Something new is making its home in the treetops—an ape.

Apes are primates. They evolved from monkeys, and like monkeys, they spend a lot of time in the trees. But unlike monkeys, apes don't have tails. And apes can move in ways monkeys can't. They can hang and swing. Sometimes they can even stand up and run on two feet, just for a moment, before getting down on all fours once more.

There's something else that makes apes special. They include your ancestors. Look closely at these apes' faces. Do they look a tiny bit familiar? They should—they're family.

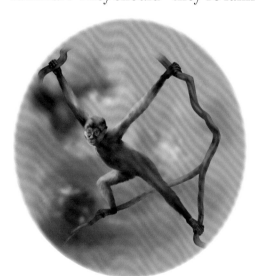

Pliopithecus and chimpanzee-faced *Proconsul* are small and monkey-like, but these tree climbers are apes, not monkeys. *Pliopithecus* is especially good at swinging from branch to branch, something no monkey can do.

▲ *Proconsul*
LENGTH: *2.5 feet*
LIVED: *19 million years ago*

▲ *Pliopithecus*
LENGTH: *2 feet*
LIVED: *14 million years ago*

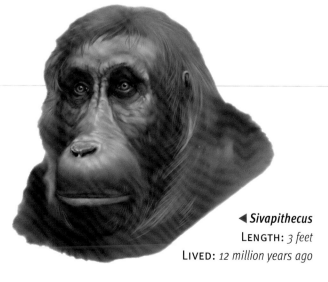

With its long face and close-together eyes, *Sivapithecus* looks like one of its closest relatives: an orangutan!

◀ *Sivapithecus*
LENGTH: *3 feet*
LIVED: *12 million years ago*

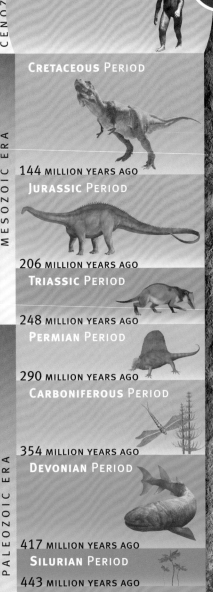

CENOZOIC ERA

QUATERNARY PERIOD
1.8 MILLION YEARS AGO
TERTIARY PERIOD

You are here

MESOZOIC ERA

CRETACEOUS PERIOD

144 MILLION YEARS AGO
JURASSIC PERIOD

206 MILLION YEARS AGO
TRIASSIC PERIOD

248 MILLION YEARS AGO
PERMIAN PERIOD

290 MILLION YEARS AGO
CARBONIFEROUS PERIOD

354 MILLION YEARS AGO
DEVONIAN PERIOD

PALEOZOIC ERA

417 MILLION YEARS AGO
SILURIAN PERIOD

443 MILLION YEARS AGO
ORDOVICIAN PERIOD

490 MILLION YEARS AGO
CAMBRIAN PERIOD

543 MILLION YEARS AGO
PRECAMBRIAN

4.5 BILLION YEARS AGO

The Human Story Begins

It's near the end of the Tertiary Period and something is moving through the tall grasses of the African savannah. At first glance, it looks like an ape. But wait; it's walking on two legs, like you. Is it a human? Not quite—but it is a very, very close relative.

The two-legged creature walking through the grass is a hominid. Guess what? So are you. Hominids are the animal group that includes not only modern humans, but also many other closely related species that are now extinct.

By traveling back in time, we can come face-to-face with a member of one of these species. This is an *Australopithecus afarensis*. She lived around three million years ago, which means she is not even the very earliest of the hominid species. The very earliest lived around eight million years ago. That's when the very first hominids evolved special features that made them different from their ape ancestors, and an entirely new type of animal climbed down from the trees and took its first steps on Earth.

▲ *Australopithecus afarensis*
HEIGHT: *3.5 feet*
LIVED: *3.2 million years ago*

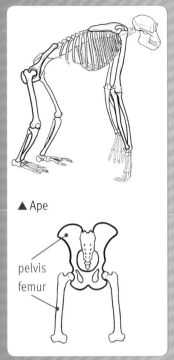

▲ Ape

pelvis

femur

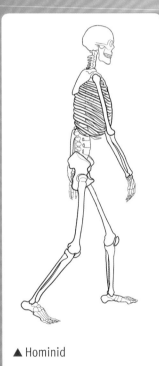

▲ Hominid

pelvis

femur

What Makes a Hominid a Hominid?

Hominids are apes. Yes, that means you, too! Just as dinosaurs are reptiles—a particular group of reptiles with unique features—hominids are a particular group of apes with unique features.

So what are those features? Well, you can probably think of a lot of things that make you different from other apes such as chimpanzees or gorillas. You can talk, dance, sing, write, draw pictures. You wear clothes, go to school and to the movies. You can do all of these things because your hominid ancestors' bodies, brains, and behaviors evolved in certain ways.

But eight million years ago, when the *very first* hominids evolved, just a few important features made them different from their ape ancestors. If we compare you to an ape, we can still see those features. Let's take a look. Let's compare a human skeleton to a chimpanzee's skeleton and see the basic things that make hominids and apes different.

What's the most important difference between hominids and other apes? Hominids are bipedal: They are built to walk on two legs all of the time. Apes can stand up sometimes, but most of the time they walk on all fours.

Here are some other differences:

TEETH
- Compared to a hominid's, an ape's canine teeth (the pointy teeth near the front of the mouth) are large.
- Compared to an ape's, a hominid's canine teeth are small.

PELVIS
- An ape's pelvis is tall and narrow.
- A hominid's shorter and wider pelvis makes for more stable walking on two legs.

TOES
- An ape's big toe is splayed off to the side, like a thumb—great for grasping, but not for bearing weight.
- A hominid's big toe is lined up with the other toes, helping to bear a bipedal body's weight.

FOOT ARCHES
- An ape's foot is flat.
- A hominid's foot is arched, absorbing shock when the foot takes a step.

FEMUR
- An ape's femur (upper leg bone) extends straight down.
- A hominid's femur angles inward, which better positions a bipedal body's knees and feet during walking. Try walking with your knees wide apart; it's hard to balance!

Your Hominid Family

Let's take another break, just for a moment, and travel again to our own time. Let's look back on the big picture of hominid evolution from a scientist's point of view.

Scientists who study hominid evolution start by looking at fossils. They look at where the fossils are found and how they are shaped. These things tell scientists some very important things about the history of human beings and our hominid relatives.

By looking at where the fossils are found, scientists can tell that the first hominids evolved in Africa and spread around the globe over time. By looking at how the fossils are shaped, scientists can tell that there have been many different species of hominid that have lived over the years. Each species has its own unique skeleton. When scientists find skulls and other bones that don't look like any others they have seen before, they know they have found another hominid species.

By looking at where these fossils are found and how they are shaped, scientists start to see the big picture. It's a picture of a planet that has not always been our own. Our own species, *Homo sapiens*, is the youngest hominid species; we have only been around for about 200,000 years or so. We are simply the latest of many species that have lived over the past eight million years.

Let's take a look at the fossil skulls and skeletons of a few of our extinct relatives. These bones tell us a lot about our hominid family.

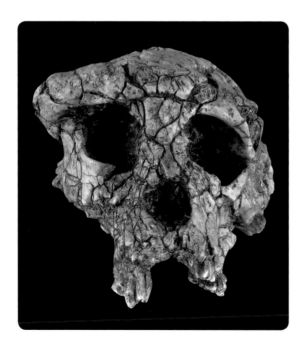

◄ *Sahelanthropus tchadensis*

Did this seven-million-year-old skull from Africa belong to an ape—or a very early hominid? *Sahelanthropus tchadensis* had a smaller brain and a big, bony brow like an ape. But its canine teeth—the pointy teeth near the front of its jaws—were smaller, like a hominid's. Is this mysterious primate a "missing link" between apes and hominids? Scientists don't yet have all the answers!

From around four million to a million years ago, different hominid species called australopithecines had evolved and were living in Africa. These early hominids walked on the ground on two legs, like we do, but they probably still spent some time in trees, like apes do. They lived alongside each other, but scientists can tell from their skulls that they had different diets: They were built for eating different types of foods.

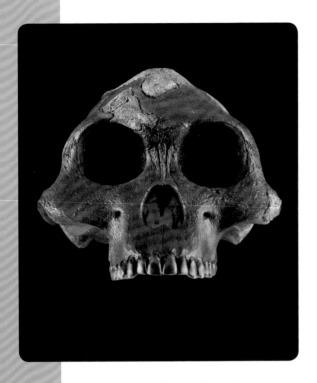

▲ *Australopithecus afarensis*

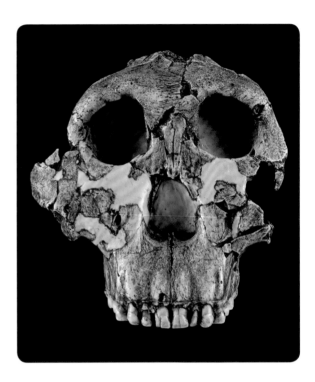

▲ *Paranthropus boisei*

The skull on the left belongs to one australopithecine. The skull on the right belongs to another. When you compare them, you notice a few things. The skull on the left is smaller, with smaller jaws and teeth. This means that this hominid was eating soft fruits and tender leaves. But the skull on the right is big and bulky, with bigger jaws and teeth. This hominid was using those teeth and jaws to chomp on hard nuts and seeds.

So what? When different species eat different things, more species can survive. If both species had evolved for the same type of diet, there might not have been enough food to go around, and one species might well have gone extinct. But when you want a banana and your neighbor wants a handful of nuts, there's no reason to fight over your dinner.

Around two and a half million years ago, some hominids evolved in Africa that looked a little bit less like apes—and more like us. They were a little bit taller, with bigger brains (like us), flatter faces (like us), and smaller teeth (like us). They were probably eating lots of different things, including meat. And unlike their earlier relatives, these hominids probably spent all of their time on the ground: Hominids had put life in the trees behind them. They were distinct species: When scientists look at their skulls and skeletons, they can see differences that tell them that these were different hominid species living alongside one another.

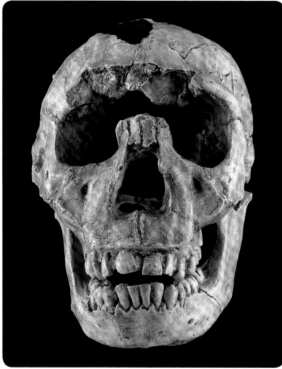

◀ *Homo ergaster*

▲ *Homo rudolfensis*

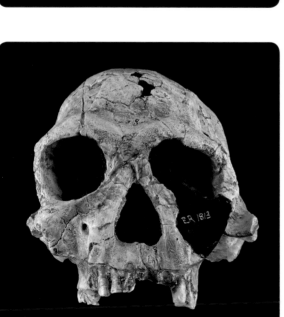

◀ *Homo habilis*

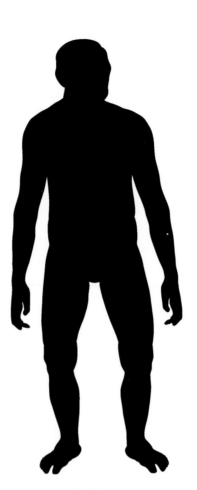

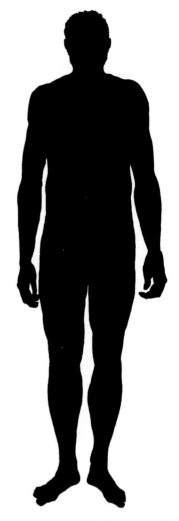

▲ Early hominids, like *Australopithecus afarensis*, were shorter than modern humans, with longer arms.

▲ Later hominids, like *Homo ergaster*, looked more like us than their earlier relatives.

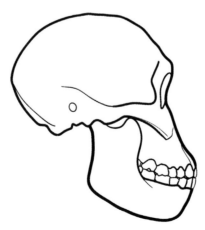

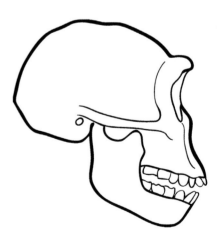

▲ Earlier hominids' skulls were more apelike.

▲ Later hominids' skulls (above) look a little bit like their ancestors' skulls, and a little bit like our skulls (right).

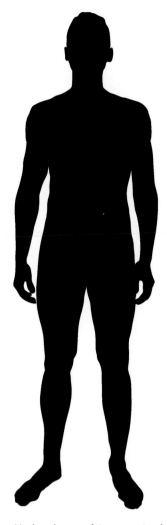

▲ Modern human (*Homo sapiens*)

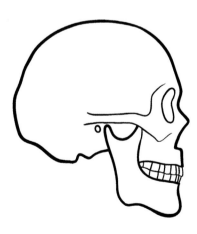

▲ Modern human

Sometime around two million years ago, hominids ventured outside Africa for the first time. Scientists have found hominid fossils in Asia and Eastern Europe that are similar to those of African hominids living at the same time. Hominids were on the move, exploring their planet and living in places no human had ever lived before.

Hominids began to explore the earth, leaving Africa for other parts of the world.

Our own species, *Homo sapiens*, first evolved in Africa around two hundred thousand years ago. Today, we are the only hominid species. But that has not always been true. Around thirty thousand years ago, the last of another species, *Homo neanderthalensis*—the Neanderthals—went extinct. For many thousands of years, the Neanderthals were our neighbors. While we spread from Africa to the rest of the world, the Neanderthals lived in Europe and western Asia. They were similar to us—but also different. While we evolved in warm Africa, they evolved in a colder part of the world. Their shorter, heavier bodies helped them to stay warm, and their long, wide noses warmed cold air when they took a breath.

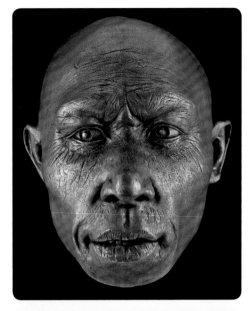

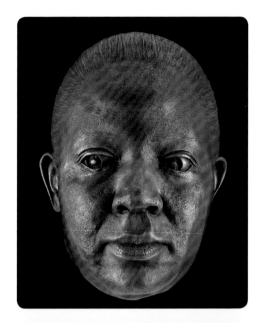

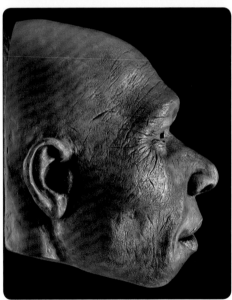

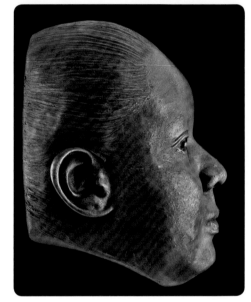

▲ A Neanderthal reconstruction

▲ A modern human reconstruction

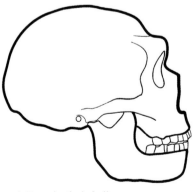

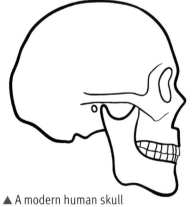

▲ A Neanderthal skull

▲ A modern human skull

Your Useless Body Parts

Ever wonder why you get goosebumps?

Scattered throughout our human bodies are parts we don't need. We carry around leftovers from our ancestors, features that helped them climb trees or stay warm or survive on a different diet from what we live on today. Though they've outlived their usefulness as we've evolved, these curious reminders of our evolutionary history have stuck around.

Some of these features can be traced back to early hominids. Some can be traced back even further, to apes, or even to early primates. Some can be traced all the way back to mammals that lived before primates even evolved. And some go back even further than that! Did you know that your human body had such a history?

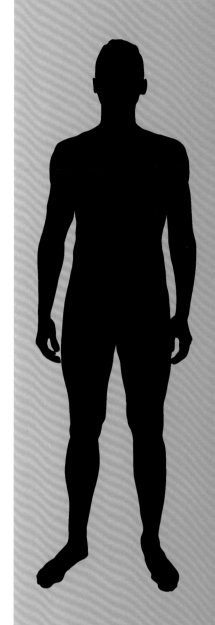

WISDOM TEETH
When your early hominid ancestors were living on plants, these extra molars came in handy. Plants provide less energy than meat, so when you live on plants, you have to do a lot of chewing to eat enough to survive.

THIRD EYELID
That tiny pink fold in the inner corner of your eye is all that's left of a membrane that helped keep your ancient ancestors' eyes clean. Reptiles have this membrane too, so we can trace it back more than three hundred million years to an ancestor we share with reptiles.

EAR WIGGLING MUSCLES
If you can wiggle your ears, it's most likely because our early primate ancestors could move their ears like dogs and cats do. By moving their ears, our ancestors could focus on sounds all around them without moving their heads.

PALMARIS MUSCLE
This long, narrow muscle that runs from wrist to elbow may have been important for climbing and hanging when your primate ancestors were tree dwellers. We don't use it anymore, and it's disappearing as we evolve; about one out of every eleven humans doesn't have it!

GOOSEBUMPS
The muscle fibers that make your hair stand on end when you're cold or scared allowed your furrier mammal ancestors to puff up to keep warm or to appear larger and more threatening to an enemy.

PINKY TOE
Your ape ancestors used all five toes for grasping or clinging to branches. Since you walk upright, your most important toe is your big toe, for balance—your smallest toe is a useless leftover.

The Geologic TIME SCALE

TODAY

You are here

CENOZOIC ERA

QUATERNARY PERIOD

TERTIARY PERIOD

65 MILLION YEARS AGO

MESOZOIC ERA

CRETACEOUS PERIOD

144 MILLION YEARS AGO

JURASSIC PERIOD

206 MILLION YEARS AGO

TRIASSIC PERIOD

248 MILLION YEARS AGO

PERMIAN PERIOD

290 MILLION YEARS AGO

PALEOZOIC ERA

CARBONIFEROUS PERIOD

354 MILLION YEARS AGO

DEVONIAN PERIOD

417 MILLION YEARS AGO

SILURIAN PERIOD

443 MILLION YEARS AGO

ORDOVICIAN PERIOD

490 MILLION YEARS AGO

CAMBRIAN PERIOD

543 MILLION YEARS AGO

PRECAMBRIAN

◀ You are here: The Quaternary Period.

▼ Massive glaciers cover much of the earth.

1.8 MILLION YEARS AGO

An Age of Ice

THE QUATERNARY PERIOD
1.8 million–10,000 years ago

A cold breeze sweeps through the valley. Under the rising moon, a group of woolly mammoths slowly marches along. An older, sickly mammoth falls behind, and humans begin their hunt. Bison munch on grass nearby. And out of the forest comes a giant bear, hot breath steaming from its wet nose.

It is a cold world, and massive glaciers cover much of the planet. The last two million years of our journey—the Quaternary Period—take place on this frigid Earth. Welcome to the ice age.

The ice age mammals you are about to meet are at once strange and familiar. You'll see fantastic saber-toothed cats, woolly elephants, and sloths as tall as a house. But you'll also see horses, dogs, and other mammals very similar to those back home in the modern world. Our journey is almost over. Life as we know it has almost arrived.

Quaternary Period, twelve thousand years ago

Tails of Two Continents

For millions and millions of years—even back to the age of dinosaurs—
North and South America were not connected. They were separated by
ocean. And on these different continents, different mammals evolved.

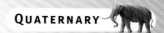

Down south, giant ground sloths, like the four-ton *Megatherium*, feed from the treetops. Meanwhile, well-armored glyptodonts—ancient relatives of modern-day armadillos—root around in the shrubbery below.

But about one million years before the Quaternary Period began, a land bridge formed between the Americas. And mammals moved. The horses, elephants, deer, cats, and dogs from the north came south, while sloths, glyptodonts, and monkeys headed north.

▲ Giant ground sloths and glyptodont

119

EVOLUTION
How It Works & How We Know
BIOGEOGRAPHY

Why do different landmasses have different species? Because each landmass—and the life that calls it home—has a different history. The study of these histories is called biogeography.

STEP 1   Let's start with a population of organisms that are all the same species, living in the same place.

STEP 2   Now, let's suppose a change in geography occurs, such as a piece of a continent splitting off to form an island.

STEP 3   Once this new landmass breaks off, the individuals on the island can end up living in conditions that are different from those they left behind.

STEP 4   Those new conditions can shape the group's evolution. For example, a predator that preyed on this species might be absent from their new home. In that case, there would be no evolutionary pressure for maintaining the defense mechanism—spiky armor, in this case—against that predator. Over generations, this can cause the trait itself to diminish.

STEP 5   The new environment might also present different food sources. Hard nuts are now everywhere! Individuals with teeth that can crack the new food thrive and pass on the trait to their offspring.

Over time, such forces can lead to changes that make the new population different from the original group back on the mainland. When the differences become great enough, the isolated population becomes a new species. And any kind of barrier—a mountain chain, a newly-formed river, or a desert—can have the same effect of isolating populations and evolving a new species out of an old one.

Mammals of the Ice Age

Bundle up! The last part of our journey is going to be cold. At the beginning of the Quaternary Period, a great ice age swept across the planet. Cooling temperatures led to heavy snows. As the snow built up, it formed massive glaciers that spread from the poles. The areas that will one day be Milwaukee and Chicago are under ice!

But mammals still thrive in these cooler climates. Lions and saber-toothed cats. Enormous, hairy elephants. The largest bears that have ever lived. It's an impressive cast of characters! Let's meet the mammals of this ice age. But please be careful. Ice age mammals can be very big, and many are deadly!

The saber-toothed cat *Smilodon* is a common ice age predator. To help survive cold weather, many mammals—such as giant ground sloths—are large and thick-skinned. But knife-like saber teeth can pierce through the thickest hides, delivering a fast and fatal wound. A tar pit, too, can be a deadly enemy, trapping both predators and their prey.

◀ *Smilodon*
LENGTH: *6 feet*
LIVED: *15,000 years ago*

▲ *Paramylodon* (ground sloth)
LENGTH: *12 feet*
LIVED: *15,000 years ago*

Lions in North America?! It's true. With big prey such as elephants, sloths, and bison around, this big cat is right at home in North America's grasslands. And if it doesn't catch you, then perhaps a pack of Dire wolves will!

▲ **American lion**
LENGTH: *7 feet*
LIVED: *15,000 years ago*

▼ **Dire wolves**
LENGTH: *4 feet*
LIVED: *15,000 years ago*

Weighing up to two thousand pounds, the mighty bear *Arctodus* is one of the largest mammal predators that has ever lived. *Arctodus* also has longer legs than other bears, so it's probably a much faster runner.

◄ *Arctodus*
LENGTH: *7 feet*
LIVED: *15,000 years ago*

With big furry coats, the closely related mammoths and mastodons are well adapted for the ice age. How are they different? Mastodons are slightly smaller, for starters, with shorter, flatter heads. Also, look at the tusks: The mammoth's tusks curve more upward and inward than those of the mastodon. And mammoths are grazers—they eat grass. Mastodons prefer leafy trees and shrubs. This means that though they were very similar animals, they were not in competition with each other for food.

▶ **Mammoth**
SHOULDER HEIGHT: *10 feet*
LIVED: *15,000 years ago*

◀ **Mastodon**
SHOULDER HEIGHT: *8 feet*
LIVED: *15,000 years ago*

◀ **Bison**
LENGTH: *8 feet*
LIVED: *15,000 years ago*

Bison first evolved in Asia near the start of the Quaternary Period. So, how did they get to North America? During the coldest times of the ice age, much of Earth's seawater is frozen into glaciers, so sea levels drop. Low sea levels expose land bridges between Siberia and Alaska, allowing animals from Asia, Europe, and Africa to travel to North America.

◀ *Equus*
LENGTH: *7 feet*
LIVED: *2.5 million years ago*

The ice age is the age of the modern horse. This species, *Equus simplicidens,* is the very first member of the genus *Equus,* to which all modern-day horses belong.

▶ *Castoroides*
LENGTH: *5 feet*
LIVED: *15,000 years ago*

Even some rodents were big during the ice age: the giant beaver *Castoroides* is as big as some bears! It's true that many ice age mammals reached massive sizes, but not everything was enormous. Smaller species—like most of the rodents—almost always outnumber the bigger ones.

Mammoths No More

What happened to the mammoths? The mastodons and saber-toothed cats? The answer: extinction. They died out. Perhaps because of climate change. Or maybe humans, who came to North America near the end of the Quaternary Period, hunted and killed them. Whatever the reason, they are gone forever. Just like the dinosaurs, trilobites, and every other organism that we saw along our journey. But just as some species die out, new ones evolve. Modern-day horses, bison, and elephants remind us of their close relatives that lived during the ice age. The legacy of the great ice age beasts—and everything that came before—lives on.

▲ Mammoths and woolly rhinos

Back Home on Our Evolving Planet

We've traveled five hundred million years since life first exploded in diversity in Earth's seas. Now we're back in our own familiar world. The animals and plants are the same ones we see around us every day.

It's a wonderful world we live in. But there's something going on that you may not have noticed before. Remember those five mass extinctions we saw on our journey? There's another one going on right now. It's harder to see it up close, when it's going on all around you. Mass extinction is a normal part of the planet's history. But this one is a little bit different. It all started about ten thousand years ago with the disappearance of mammoths, mastodons, and other big mammals. Early on, climate change may have been the cause. But today, we play an important part. For the first time in Earth's history, species are dying out because of things that human beings are doing. The Tasmanian wolf, the passenger pigeon, the broad-billed parrot, the sea mink, the moa. These are just a few of the species we've driven to extinction in the last few hundred years.

We humans can do amazing things. No other animal can paint a picture, or write a poem, or plant a tree. Unfortunately, some of the things we do are hard on the planet. We drive cars that pollute the atmosphere. We cut down forests that other animals call home. By doing these things, we are causing many species to go extinct. The good news is, because we are human beings, we have the ability to figure out how to make changes that can make a difference.

Human beings evolved in the same way all other animals evolved. Even so, we are unique. We have the ability to study and understand the planet's diversity. We are also a part of the planet's diversity. We are one species of the millions that have lived on Earth since life first appeared almost four billion years ago. As we tell the story of our evolving planet, we can also remember that we are simply one part of that story.

And that's pretty amazing.

"[F]rom so simple a beginning, endless forms most beautiful and most wonderful have been, and are being, evolved."

—CHARLES DARWIN

Pronunciation Key

Acanthostega (uh-KAN-tho-STEG-uh)
Acheloma (AK-ee-LO-muh)
Acrothyra (AK-ro-THY-ruh)
Allophylus (AL-o-FY-lus)
Allosaurus (AL-o-SOR-us)
Amia (AY-mee-uh)
Ammonoid (AM-uh-noyd)
Anchiceratops (AN-kee-SAIR-uh-tops)
Andalgalornis (AN-dul-gal-OR-nis)
Angiosperm (AN-gee-oh-spurm)
Angistorhinus (AN-ghis-toh-RY-nus)
Ankylosaur (an-KY-luh-sor)
Annelid (AN-uh-lid)
Annularia (AN-ew-LAIR-ee-uh)
Anomalocaris (an-OM-uh-loh-KAIR-us)
Apatosaurus (uh-PAT-uh-SOR-us)
Archaeanthus (AR-kee-AN-thus)
Archaeotherium
    (AR-kee-o-THEER-ee-um)
Arctodus (ark-TOH-dus)
Arthropod (AR-thruh-pod)
Asterotrygon (AS-ter-oh-TRY-gon)
Augustasaurus (uh-GUS-tuh-SOR-us)
Aulacephalodon
    (AW-luh-SEF-uh-luh-don)
Australopithecine
    (OS-tray-loh-PITH-uh-seen)
Australopithecus afarensis (OS-tray-loh-
    PITH-uh-kus AF-uh-REN-sis)
Bandringa (ban-DRING-guh)
Barylambda (BAIR-ee-LAM-duh)
Bathyuriscus (BATH-ee-uh-RIS-kus)
Belemnite (buh-LEM-nite)
Belemnitella (BEL-um-nih-TELL-uh)
Brachiopod (BRAK-ee-oh-pod)
Brachiosaurus (BRAK-ee-oh-SOR-us)
Bradysaurus (BRAY-dee-SOR-us)
Cacops (KAY-kops)
Calamites (KAL-uh-MY-teez)
Cambrian (KAYM-bree-un)
Canadia (kuh-NAY-dee-uh)
Canine (KAY-nyn)
Capsospongia (KAP-soh-SPUN-jee-uh)
Captorhinus (KAP-toh-RY-nus)
Carboniferous (KAR-boh-NIF-uh-rus)
Carnivoran (kar-NIV-uh-run)
Casea (kay-SEE-uh)
Castoroides (KAS-tur-OY-deez)
Cenozoic (SEN-oh-ZOH-ik)
Chalicothere (kuh-LEE-koh-theer)
Chancelloria (CHAN-suh-LOR-ree-uh)
Chordate (KOR-dayt)
Cladophlebis (KLAY-doh-FLEB-is)
Cnidarian (ny-DAIR-ee-un)
Coccosteus (ko-KOS-tee-us)
Conifer (KON-if-ur)
Coryphodon (kor-EEF-o-don)
Craumauchenia
    (KRAU-mau-CHEN-ee-uh)
Cretaceous (kreh-TAY-shus)
Crossopholis (kros-OFF-uh-lis)
Cryolophosaurus (KRY-o-LO-fo-SOR-us)
Cycad (SY-kad)
Cynodont (SY-noh-dont)
Daspletosaurus
    (duh-SPLEE-toh-SOR-us)

Deinonychus (dy-NON-ih-kus)
Devonian (deh-VO-nee-un)
Diadectes (DY-uh-DEK-teez)
Diagoniella (dy-AG-un-ee-EL-uh)
Diapsid (dy-AP-sid)
Dibothrosuchus (DY-bo-thro-SOO-kus)
Didymictis (DID-ee-MIK-tus)
Dimetrodon (dy-MEE-tro-don)
Dinictis (din-IK-tis)
Diplacanthus (DIP-luh-KAN-thus)
Diplocaulus (DIP-lo-KAHL-us)
Diraphora (DY-ruh-FOR-uh)
Dunkleosteus (DUNK-lee-OS-tee-us)
Echinoderm (ee-KY-no-durm)
Edaphosaurus (ee-DAF-uh-SOR-us)
Edmontonia (ed-mun-TO-nee-uh)
Eiffelia (i-FEL-ee-uh)
Eldonia (el-DOH-nee-uh)
Endoceras (en-DAH-sur-us)
Eobasileus (EE-oh-buh-SIL-ee-us)
Equus simplicidens
    (EK-wus sim-PLIH-sih-denz)
Eryops (AIR-ee-ops)
Esox (EE-soks)
Eubleptus (you-BLEP-tus)
Favistina (FAV-ih-STEE-nuh)
Ginkgo (GING-koh)
Glyptodont (GLIP-toh-dont)
Gogia (GOH-jee-uh)
Gomphotherium
    (GOM-pho-THEER-ee-um)
Guembelastraea
    (GWEM-buh-luh-STRAY-uh)
Hallucigenia
    (huh-LOO-sih-JEE-nee-uh)
Helicoprion (hee-luh-KO-pree-on)
Hesperocyon (HES-pur-o-SY-on)
Herrerasaurus (huh-REHR-uh-SOR-us)
Holocene (HOL-o-seen)
Homalodotherium
    (HOM-uh-luh-do-THEER-ee-um)
Hominid (HOM-uh-nid)
Homo ergaster (HO-mo ur-GAS-ter)
Homo habilis (HO-mo HAB-ih-lus)
Homo neanderthalensis
    (HO-mo nee-AN-der-tahl-EN-sis)
Homo rudolfensis
    (HO-mo ROO-dolf-EN-sis)
Homo sapiens (HO-mo SAY-pee-uns)
Hoplophoneus (HOP-lo-FO-nee-us)
Hyracotherium
    (hy-RAK-oh-THEER-ee-um)
Icaronycteris (IK-uh-ro-nik-TAIR-us)
Ichthyosaur (IK-thee-oh-sor)
Incisor (in-SY-zur)
Isalorhynchus (eye-SAY-lo-RING-kus)
Isotelus (EYE-so-TAY-lus)
Jonkeria (yon-KAIR-ee-uh)
Jurassic (ju-RASS-ik)
Knightia (NY-tee-uh)
Labidosaurus (LAB-ih-doh-SOR-us)
Lambeosaurus (LAM-ee-oh-SOR-us)
Leidyosuchus (LY-dee-o-SOO-kus)
Lepidodendron (LEP-ee-doh-DEN-drun)
Lufengosaurus (loo-FENG-go-SOR-us)
Lycaenops (LY-kun-ops)

Mackenzia (muh-KEN-zee-uh)
Mahajangasuchus
    (MAH-ha-JANG-guh-SOO-kus)
Majungasaurus (muh-JUNG-ga-SOR-us)
Marginocephalian
    (MAR-jin-o-suh-FAY-lee-un)
Marrella (muh-REL-uh)
Marsupial (mar-SOO-pee-ul)
Masillosteus (maz-il-OS-tee-us)
Megatherium (MEG-uh-THEER-ee-um)
Menodus (men-O-dus)
Mesohippus (MEZ-o-HIP-us)
Mesosaurus (MEE-so-SOR-us)
Mesozoic (MEZ-o-ZO-ik)
Micromitra (MY-kro-MEE-tra)
Mioplosus (MY-o-PLO-sus)
Mollusk (MOL-usk)
Morganucodon (MOR-guh-NOO-ko-don)
Moropus (mor-O-pus)
Mortoniceras (MOR-ton-uh-SAIR-us)
Mosasaur (MO-zuh-SOR)
Neanderthal (nee-AN-der-tahl)
Neuropteris (nur-OP-tur-us)
Nisusia (nih-SOOS-ee-uh)
Notharctus (no-THARK-tus)
Nyctosaurus (NIK-toh-SOR-us)
Odaraia (oh-DAR-ee-uh)
Omnivore (OM-ni-vor)
Opabinia (OH-puh-BIN-ee-uh)
Ophiacodon (OH-fee-AK-o-don)
Ordovician (OR-doh-VISH-ee-un)
Ornithopod (or-NITH-o-pod)
Osteoderm (OS-tee-o-durm)
Oxydactylus (OX-ee-DAK-tuh-lus)
Palaeoniscum (PAY-lee-o-NIS-kum)
Paleozoic (PAY-lee-o-ZOH-ik)
Palmaris (pahl-MAIR-is)
Pantodont (PAN-toh-dont)
Pantylus (pan-TY-lus)
Paramylodon (PAIR-uh-MY-luh-don)
Paramys (PAIR-uh-mees)
Paranthropus boisei
    (PAIR-an-THROP-us BOYZ-ee-eye)
Parasaurolophus
    (PAIR-uh-sor-AH-luh-fus)
Paroodectes (PAIR-oh-DEK-teez)
Pecopteris (pee-KOP-tur-is)
Perchoerus (pur-KAIR-us)
Permian (PUR-mee-un)
Phareodus (FAIR-ee-OH-dus)
Pholidophrus (FO-lid-O-fruhs)
Phylogeny (fy-LAH-jin-ee)
Pikaia (pih-KY-uh)
Pirania (pih-RAHN-ee-uh)
Platanus (plih-TAIN-us)
Platecarpus (PLAT-uh-KAR-pus)
Platystrophia (PLAT-is-TRO-fee-uh)
Plegiocidaris (PLEE-jee-o-sih-DAIR-us)
Pleurotomaria
    (PLUR-o-toh-MAR-ee-uh)
Pliohippus (PLY-o-HIP-us)
Pliopithecus (PLY-o-PITH-uh-kus)
Poriferan (por-IF-uh-run)
Precambrian (pree-CAIM-bree-un)
Primate (PRY-mait)
Priscacara (PRIS-kuh-KAR-uh)

Proconsul (pro-KUN-sul)
Prosauropod (pro-SOR-uh-pod)
Protaspis (pro-TAS-pis)
Protoceratops (pro-to-SAIR-uh-tops)
Protorothyris (pro-tuh-ro-THY-ris)
Pterosaur (TAIR-uh-sor)
Quaternary (kwa-TUR-nur-ee)
Rhamphorhynchus (RAM-for-ING-kus)
Rapetosaurus (ruh-PAY-toh-SOR-us)
Sabalites (SAB-uh-LY-teez)
Sahelanthropus (SAH-heel-AN-thro-
    pus)
Saniwa (san-EE-wah)
Sauropod (SOR-o-pod)
Sauropterygian (sor-OP-tur-ID-jee-un)
Scenella (sen-EL-uh)
Seymouria (see-MOR-ee-uh)
Silurian (sil-UR-ee-un)
Simosuchus (SEE-mo-SOO-kus)
Sinornithosaurus
    (sy-NOR-nith-o-SOR-us)
Sivapithecus (SEE-vuh-PITH-uh-kus)
Smilodon (SMY-lo-don)
Stegoceras (steg-OS-ur-us)
Stegosaurus (STEG-o-SOR-us)
Steneosaurus (STEE-nee-o-SOR-us)
Stenopterygius (sten-OP-tur-ID-jee-us)
Sterculia (stur-KOOL-ee-uh)
Stethacanthus (STETH-uh-KAN-thus)
Streptelasma (STREP-tuh-LAZ-muh)
Symmorium (sim-OR-ee-um)
Synapsid (sin-AP-sid)
Teleoceras (TEE-lee-uh-SUR-us)
Tertiary (TUR-shee-air-ee)
Tetrapod (TET-ruh-pod)
Thalassomedon (thuh-LAS-o-muh-don)
Theropod (THAIR-o-pod)
Thrinaxodon (thrin-AX-o-don)
Thylacosmilus (THY-lak-o-SMY-lus)
Thyreophoran (THY-ree-o-FOR-un)
Tiktaalik (tik-TAH-lik)
Titanothere (ty-TAN-o-theer)
Toxochelys (TOX-o-KEE-lis)
Triassic (try-AS-ic)
Triceratops (try-SAIR-uh-tops)
Trigonias (trig-O-nee-us)
Trilobite (TRY-lo-byt)
Typha (TY-fuh)
Tyrannosaurus (tuh-RAN-o-SOR-us)
Uintathere (yoo-IN-tuh-theer)
Urasterella (yoo-RAS-tur-EL-uh)
Varanops (VAIR-uh-nops)
Vauxia (VOX-ee-uh)
Vertebrate (VUR-tuh-brut)
Wiwaxia (wih-WAX-ee-uh)
Xenocrinus (ZEE-no-KRY-nus)
Xiphactinus (zy-FAK-tin-us)
Youngina (yung-GY-nuh)

Glossary

Algae – Plant-like organisms that use the sun's energy to make food. Land plants evolved from a type of algae during the Ordovician Period. Seaweed and kelp are types of algae.

Amniotes – Tetrapods with eggs that are "water-tight" and resistant to drying out. Reptiles and synapsids are the two types of amniotes.

Amphibians – Tetrapods with soft eggs that will dry out if not laid in water. Frogs and salamanders are types of amphibians.

Angiosperms – Plants with flowers and fruit.

Annelids – Worms with "ringed" bodies made up of multiple segments. Worms are invertebrate animals; earthworms are a type of annelid worm.

Arthropods – Invertebrate animals with jointed legs and bodies covered by a hard outer skeleton. Insects, spiders, and trilobites are types of arthropods.

Australopithecines – Early hominids that had large teeth, small brains, and other ape-like features. Australopithecines lived from around four million to one million years ago. *Australopithecus* and *Paranthropus* are types of australopithecines.

Bacteria – Single-celled organisms with round, spiral, or rod-shaped forms. Bacteria can live singly or in a chain with other bacteria.

Biogeography – The science that studies the history of landmasses and the life on them.

Birds – Theropod dinosaurs with arms longer than legs. Many birds can fly.

Bone – Hard tissue that forms the skeletons of most vertebrates.

Brachiopods – Invertebrate animals that have two shells, such as clams, but one shell is bigger than the other. Brachiopods open their shells and use hair-like structures to draw water and food into their gut.

Cambrian Period – The period of Earth's history from 543 to 490 million years ago. It was during the Cambrian Period that arthropods, echinoderms, sponges, and almost all other major animal groups first evolved. Trilobites are very common.

Carboniferous Period – The period of Earth's history from 354 to 290 million years ago. During the Carboniferous Period, Pangaea began to form, ice caps covered the south pole, and vast tropical forests spread across the land at the equator.

Carnivorans – Mammals with scissor-like teeth for slicing meat. Cats, dogs, seals, and bears are types of carnivorans.

Carnivore – An animal that eats meat.

Cartilage – The tough, elastic tissue common in the bodies of many vertebrates. The skeletons of sharks (and the tip of your nose!) are made of cartilage.

Cell – The basic unit of all organisms. All cells contain the basic materials needed for life.

Cenozoic Era – The part of Earth's history that began 65 million years ago and continues today. The Cenozoic Era is made up of the Tertiary and Quaternary periods.

Chalicotheres – An extinct group of plant-eating mammals that had long front legs with large front claws for reaching up and bringing down a leafy bite. Chalicotheres lived during the Tertiary Period and the early part of the Quaternary Period.

Chordates – Animals with a nerve cord that sits on top of a tough but flexible rod called a notochord. Vertebrates are a type of chordate in which a backbone forms around the notochord. Fish, lizards, and humans are types of chordates.

Cnidarians – Invertebrate animals with stinging cells used to poison predators or prey. Jellyfish and corals are types of cnidarians.

Convergent evolution – When different species evolve similar features because they face similar environmental challenges. For example, *Thylacosmilus* and *Hoplophoneus* are two different mammals that both evolved long saber teeth for killing big prey.

Cretaceous Period – The period of Earth's history from 144 to 65 million years ago. Dinosaurs continued to rule the land, while mosasaurs hunted the seas. The first plants with flowers evolved. But at the end of the Cretaceous, a mass extinction wiped out 50 percent of all species, including all dinosaurs except birds.

Cynodont – Synapsids that have heels on their feet and a palate separating the nasal passage from the mouth. Mammals are a special type of cynodont.

Devonian Period – The period of Earth's history from 417 to 354 million years ago. Fishes are common in Devonian seas. Up on land, plants with pollen and seeds first evolved. And at the shores, the first tetrapods evolved. A mass extinction wiped out 70 percent of species at the end of the Devonian Period.

Diapsids – Reptiles that have two openings in their skull behind each eye socket. Crocodiles, lizards, and dinosaurs are types of diapsids.

Dinosaurs – Diapsid reptiles whose legs extend straight down underneath their body, not sprawling out to the side like a crocodile or lizard. Dinosaurs first evolved in the Triassic Period. Birds are the only dinosaurs that survive today.

DNA – Deoxyribonucleic acid, an organic compound. It contains the "instructions" for cells to grow and function. A cell passes along a copy of its DNA to its offspring during reproduction.

Echinoderms – Invertebrate animals with inner skeletons made of hard plates and usually covered with spines. Starfish, sea urchins, and sea cucumbers are types of echinoderms.

Embryo – Any animal or plant in an early stage of growth.

Equator – An imaginary line on the earth's surface halfway between the North and South poles, dividing the planet into the Northern and Southern hemispheres.

Evolution – The process of life changing over time.

Extinction – When a species dies out forever.

Fossil – The remains or traces of organisms that were once alive. Dinosaur bones, ammonoid shells, mammoth hair, and footprints of ancient amphibians are types of fossils.

Fossilization – The process of turning a dead organism into a fossil.

Gene – The unit of heredity.

Geologic Time Scale – Earth's history as divided by scientists into eras, periods, and other smaller chunks of time.

Glacier – A mass of ice—on land—that moves. Glaciers form when snow falls and piles up on other snow; the snow is compacted to form ice.

Glyptodonts – An extinct group of mammals that had large, bony shells on their bodies. Glyptodonts are ancient relatives of today's armadillos.

Herbivore – An animal that eats plants.

Hominid – A type of ape that walks upright on two legs and has small canine teeth (the pointy teeth near the front of the mouth). Humans are a type of hominid!

Homo – Hominids that have smaller teeth, larger brains, and flatter faces than the early australopithecines. The first species of *Homo* evolved around two and a half million years ago. *Homo habilis*, *Homo ergaster*, *Homo neanderthalensis*, and *Homo sapiens* (modern-day humans) are types of *Homo*.

Hoof – A wide bone at the end of a toe that has a thick covering of keratin (the same material that makes up your fingernails).

Ice age – A long time—thousands or millions of years—when conditions are cold enough that large masses of ice form and stay on the planet.

Ichthyosaurs – Swimming reptiles that looked similar to today's dolphins. Ichthyosaurs lived during the Mesozoic Era. *Stenopterygius* is a type of ichthyosaur.

Insects – Arthropods that have six jointed legs (three pairs) and bodies with three parts (head, thorax, and abdomen). Insects first evolved in the Silurian Period.

Invertebrate – An animal that does not have a backbone. Squids, sponges, and insects are types of invertebrates.

Jurassic Period – The period of Earth's history from 206 to 144 million years ago. During the Jurassic Period, dinosaurs dominated the land, the first birds appeared, and Pangaea began to break apart as the Atlantic Ocean began to form.

Mammals – Cynodont synapsids that have hair; the ability to suckle their young; three bones in the middle ear; and a mouth equipped with different kinds of teeth for different jobs. Mammals first evolved in the Triassic Period. Platypuses, kangaroos, elephants, and humans are types of mammals living today.

Mammoths – Large elephants that were common during the last ice age. Unlike mastodons, which fed on leafy trees and shrubs, mammoths ate grasses. Both mammoths and mastodons became extinct around ten thousand years ago.

Marginocephalians – Plant-eating dinosaurs that have a "frill" of bone at the back of the skull.

Triceratops, *Protoceratops*, and *Stegoceras* are types of marginocephalians.

Marsupials – Mammals that are born early and then often continue to develop in a pouch. Koalas and kangaroos are types of marsupials.

Mass extinction – A period of time—thousands or millions of years—when many species go extinct across much of the world. There have been five mass extinctions during the history of life on Earth. A sixth mass extinction is happening right now.

Mastodons – Large elephants that were common during the last ice age. Unlike mammoths, which fed on grasses, mastodons ate leafy trees and shrubs. Both mastodons and mammoths became extinct around ten thousand years ago.

Mesozoic Era – The part of Earth's history from 248 to 65 million years ago. The Mesozoic Era is made up of the Triassic, Jurassic, and Cretaceous periods.

Mollusks – Invertebrate animals that have a muscular "foot" used to move or grasp prey. Clams, snails, squids, and slugs are types of mollusks.

Mosasaurs – Sleek, swimming reptiles that were common during the Cretaceous Period. Mosasaurs are a type of lizard that evolved to live in the seas. *Platecarpus* is a type of mosasaur.

Natural selection – The process that leads to evolution. When an individual of a species has features that make it more likely to survive, it's more likely to reproduce and pass on the genes for those features to the next generation.

Neanderthals – Hominid species that lived in Europe and Asia from around 400,000 to 30,000 years ago. The species name for Neanderthals is *Homo neanderthalensis*.

Omnivore – An animal that eats both meat and plants.

Ordovician Period – The period of Earth's history from 490 to 443 million years ago. The seas were full of trilobites, brachiopods, starfish, corals, and other animals during this period. But at the end of the period, a mass extinction wiped out 70 percent of all species. On land, the very first land plants were starting to evolve from algae.

Organism – Any living thing, from bacteria to plants to dinosaurs to you.

Ornithopods – Plant-eating dinosaurs that were very common during the Cretaceous Period. *Parasaurolophus* and *Lambeosaurus* are types of ornithopods.

Paleozoic Era – The part of Earth's history from 543 to 248 million years ago. The Paleozoic Era is made up of the Cambrian, Ordovician, Silurian, Devonian, Carboniferous, and Permian Periods.

Pangaea – The single landmass that formed when all of the continents came together. Pangaea started to form during the Carboniferous Period, reached its greatest size during the Triassic Period, and then started to break up during the Jurassic Period.

Pantodonts – An extinct group of large, plant-eating mammals that lived during the Tertiary Period. *Barylambda* and *Coryphodon* are types of pantodonts.

Permian Period – The period of Earth's history from 290 to 248 million years ago. During the Permian Period, amphibians, reptiles, and synapsids were common across Pangaea. But at the end of the Permian, the most devastating mass extinction in Earth's history wiped out more than 90 percent of animals in the waters and 80 percent of animals on land.

Phylogeny – The evolutionary history of any group of organisms.

Poriferans – Invertebrate animals that circulate water through pores in their bodies to eat tiny water-dwelling organisms. Poriferans are also known as sponges.

Precambrian – The part of Earth's history from the formation of the planet 4.5 billion years ago to the beginning of the Paleozoic Era 543 million years ago. That's 90 percent of the planet's history! Life during most of the Precambrian was made up of small, single-celled organisms.

Primates – Mammals that have grasping hands and feet, forward-facing eyes, and a large brain. Lemurs, monkeys, and apes—including you—are types of primates.

Prosauropods – Planet-eating dinosaurs with long necks that could stand up on two legs or walk on all fours. Sauropod dinosaurs evolved from prosauropods.

Pterosaurs – Flying reptiles with wings made from skin that attached to their arms and one long finger on each hand. Pterosaurs are diapsid reptiles. They first evolved in the Triassic Period, but went extinct at the end of the Cretaceous Period.

Quaternary Period – The period of Earth's history that began 1.8 million years ago and continues today. The Quaternary Period is also known as the time of the current ice age. Our own species, *Homo sapiens*, first evolved during the Quaternary.

Reptiles – Amniotes that never have just a single opening in the skull just behind each eye socket (like synapsids). Instead, some reptiles have two openings there, some have none, and some do have just one, but in other parts of the skull. Crocodiles, lizards, and dinosaurs are types of reptiles.

Rodents – Mammals with large incisors—the teeth at the front of the mouth—that never stop growing. Squirrels and beavers are types of rodents.

Sauropods – Planet-eating dinosaurs with long necks. *Apatosaurus*, *Brachiosaurus*, and *Rapetosaurus* are types of sauropods.

Sauropterygians – A group of swimming reptiles that lived during the Mesozoic Era. Many had long, snake-like necks. *Augustasaurus* and *Thalassomedon* are types of sauropterygians.

Silurian Period – The period of Earth's history from 443 to 417 million years ago. During the Silurian Period, the planet started turning green as plants spread across the land. And insects first evolved!

Species – A group of organisms of exactly the same type, such as grizzly bears, or red-winged blackbirds, or *Tyrannosaurus rex*. The modern species of human—your species—is *Homo sapiens*.

Synapsids – Amniotes that have a single opening in the skull just behind each eye socket. Sail backs such as *Dimetrodon* are synapsids. And so are mammals!

Tertiary Period – The period of Earth's history from 65 to 1.8 million years ago. It was during the Tertiary Period that many of the mammal groups we know today—apes, elephants, horses, cats, dogs—first evolved. Our own human family also first appeared during the Tertiary.

Tetrapods – Vertebrate animals with four limbs (arms and legs) and digits (fingers and toes). Tetrapods first evolved during the Devonian Period.

Theory – An explanation that is supported by evidence and repeatedly stands up when put to the test. A theory is *not* simply a hunch or best guess.

Theropods – The meat-eating dinosaurs. *Tyrannosaurus*, *Allosaurus*, and *Deinonychus* are types of theropods. And so are birds!

Thyreophorans – Plant-eating dinosaurs that have rows of bony plates, called osteoderms, on their bodies. *Stegosaurus* and *Edmontonia* are types of thyreophorans.

Titanotheres – Large, rhinoceros-like mammals that lived during the Tertiary Period. *Menodus* is a type of titanothere.

Triassic Period – The period of Earth's history from 248 to 206 million years ago. Mammals, dinosaurs, pterosaurs, crocodiles, lizards, and turtles first evolved during the Triassic Period, and Pangaea reached its largest size. A mass extinction at the end of the Triassic wiped out many tetrapods, land plants, and animals in the seas.

Trilobites – Arthropods with bodies divided into three lobes, or segments—one lobe down the middle and an outer lobe on each side. Trilobites first evolved during the Cambrian Period; they became extinct at the end of the Permian Period. Trilobites were among the first animals with eyes!

Uintatheres – An extinct group of plant-eating mammals that lived during the Tertiary Period and had large knobs sticking out from their skulls. *Eobasileus* is a type of uintathere.

Vertebrate – An animal that has a backbone, which can be made of cartilage or bone. Vertebrates first evolved during the Cambrian Period. Fish, dinosaurs, and mammals are types of vertebrates.

Illustration Credits

All images are listed left to right and top to bottom unless otherwise indicated.

Artwork by Kalliopi Monoyios
Page 28 top

Courtesy of the Darwin Heirlooms Trust, © English Heritage Photo Library
Page 51

Karen Carr Studio (www.karencarr.com)
Pages 80–81 New Mexico Extinction Mural

National Park Service, Harpers Ferry Center, artist Robert Hynes
Page 87 top and middle

Photograph courtesy of Dr. Lance Grande
Page 87 bottom

Photographs courtesy of Jack Wittry
Pages 36–37

Paleogeographic maps by C. R. Scotese, © 2007, PALEOMAP Project (www.scotese.com)
Pages 12, 22, 30, 38, 52, 82, 113, 116

© The Field Museum
Page 72 GEO85802c. Pages 112–113 silhouettes; page 115; artwork by Kacey Ballard. Page 44 skulls 2–4; page 46 skull; page 108; pages 112–113 skulls; page 114 skulls; artwork by Gretchen Baker. Pages 20, 50, 56, 104, 120, artwork by Pat Bradley. Pages 64–65 GN89907c, artwork by John Gurche. Pages 8, 12, 21, 22, 29, 30, 35, 38, 49, 52, 60, 80, 82, 106, 116, artwork by David Quednau. Page 89 GEO86416_040d, GEO86416_062d, GEO86416_089d; page 90 GEO86416_064d, GEO86416_099d, GEO86416_106d; page 91 GEO86416_123d, GEO86416_130d; page 92 GEO86416_095d, GEO86416_072d, GEO86416_051d, GEO86416_104d; page 93 GEO86416_002d, GEO86454_03d, GEO86416_022d; page 94 GEO86416_111d, GEO86416_128d, GEO86416_034d; page 95 GEO86416_134d, GEO86416_112d; page 96 GEO86416_133d, GEO86416_053d, GEO86416_119d; page 97 GEO86416_003d, GEO86416_007d, GEO86416_025d, GEO86416_029d, GEO86416_054d, GEO86416_083d; photographer Dov Scher. Page 91 GEO85312c; photographer Ron Testa. Page 34 GEO85637c; page 55 top GEO86427_04d; page 57 (sculpture by Stephen Czerkas) GEO85843_4c; page 88 GEO86452_02d; spine and page 107 (sculpture by Elisabeth Daynes) GN90846_158d; page 109 A114414_13d; page 110 A114414_10d, A114414_07d; page 111 A114414_09d, A114414_012d, A114414_06d; page 114 (sculpture by Elisabeth Daynes) A114423_05d, A114423_11d, A114423_06d, A114423_14d; photographer John Weinstein.

© The Field Museum, artwork by Karen Carr
Front cover (counterclockwise from top left) images 1–2 GEO86500d_JuCrPF01_i11-2, GEO86500d_Te1PF01_i5; images 4–7 GEO86500d_JuCrPF11_i8, GEO86500d_SiDePF02_i3, GEO86500d_QuPP01_i1, GEO86500d_TrPP01_i1 (detail); front flap GEO86500d_CbPmPF04_i15; frontispiece (counterclockwise

from top right) images 1–5 GEO86500d_Te1PF01_i3, GEO86500d_SiDePF02_i6, GEO86500d_JuCrPF05_i5, GEO86500d_Te2PF02_Gomphotherium, GEO86500d_CbPmPF05_i2; contents GEO86500d_CbPmPF05_i9; acknowledgments GEO86500d_TrPPF02_i2; foreword image 2 GEO86500d_QuPF05_i2; pages 10–11 GEO86500d_PrePP01_i1; pages 12–13 GEO86500d_CmOr.PP.01_i1; pages 22–23 GEO86500d_SiDe.PP.01_i1; page 24 GEO86500d_SiDePF02_i1, GEO86500d_SiDePF02_i3; page 25 GEO86500d_SiDePF02_i2, GEO86500d_SiDePF02_i12, GEO86500d_SiDePF02_i4; page 28 bottom GEO86500d_Acanthostega; pages 30–31 GEO86500d_CbPmPP01_i1; page 32 GEO86500d_SiDePF02_i9, GEO86500d_SiDePF02_i10; page 33 GEO86500d_SiDePF02_i6, GEO86500d_SiDePF02_i7, GEO86500d_SiDePF02_i8; page 38–39 GEO86500d_CbPmPP02_i1; page 40 GEO86500d_CbPmPF04_i1, GEO86500d_CbPmPF04_i2; page 41 GEO86500d_CbPmPF04_i3, GEO86500d_CbPmPF04_i8, GEO86500d_CbPmPF04_i6; page 42 GEO86500d_CbPmPF04_i4, GEO86500d_Diadectes; page 43 GEO86500d_CbPmPF05_i5, GEO86500d_CbPmPF05_i4; page 44 skull 1 &5; page 45 GEO86500d_CbPmPF05_i1, GEO86500d_CbPmPF05_i16, GEO86500d_CbPmPF05_i2; page 46 GEO86500d_CbPmPF05_i3, GEO86500d_CbPmPF05_i8, GEO86500d_CbPmPF05_i6; page 47 GEO86500d_CbPmPF04_i10, GEO86500d_CbPmPF05_i9, GEO86500d_CbPmPF05_i7; page 48 GEO86500d_CbPmPF04_i14, GEO86500d_CbPmPF04_i12, GEO86500d_CbPmPF04_i13, GEO86500d_CbPmPF04_i15; pages 52–53 GEO86500d_TrPP01_i1; page 54 GEO86500d_CbPmPF04_i10, GEO86500d_CbPmPF04_i14, GEO86500d_CbPmPF04_i15; page 55 bottom GEO86500d_TrPF03_i1; page 58 GEO86500d_CbPmPF05_i3, GEO86500d_TrPF02_i1, GEO86500d_TrPF02_i2; page 59 GEO86500d_JuCrPF07_i1, GEO86500d_JuCrPF05_i5, GEO86500d_Daspletosaurus; page 61 GEO86500d_JuCrPF04_i1, GEO86500d_JuCrPF04_i3; page 62 GEO86500d_JuCrPF05_i5; page 63 GEO86500d_JuCrPF05_i1, GEO86500d_JuCrPF05_i6, GEO86500d_JuCrPF05_i2; page 66 GEO86500d_JuCrPF06_i2, GEO86500d_Daspletosaurus, GEO86500d_JuCrPF06_i4; page 67 GEO86500d_JuCrPF06_i3, GEO86500d_JuCrPF03_i1, GEO86500d_JuCrPF10_i3; page 69 GEO86500d_JuCrPF07_i1, GEO86500d_JuCrPF06_i1; page 70 GEO86500d_JuCrPF08_i2; page 71 GEO86500d_JuCrPF08_i1, GEO86500d_JuCrPF08_i3, GEO86500d_JuCrPF08_i5; page 73 GEO86500d_JuCrPF11_i3, GEO86500d_JuCrPF11_i4; page 74 GEO86500d_JuCrPF11_i5, GEO86500d_JuCrPF11_i6, GEO86500d_JuCrPF11_i10; page 75 GEO86500d_JuCrPF11_i8, GEO86500d_JuCrPF11_i7; page 76 GEO86500d_JuCrPF01_i3, GEO86500d_JuCrPF01_i10, GEO86500d_JuCrPF01_i9; page 77 GEO86500d_JuCrPF01_i6, GEO86500d_JuCrPF01_i13, GEO86500d_JuCrPF01_i8, GEO86500d_JuCrPF01_i12; page 78 GEO86500d_JuCrPF01_i1, GEO86500d_Thalassomedon; page 79 GEO86500d_JuCrPF01_i7, GEO86500d_JuCrPF01_i11; pages 82–83 GEO86500d_Te1.PP.01_i1; page 84 GEO86500d_Te1PF01_i1, GEO86500d_Te1PF01_i2; page 85 GEO86500d_

Te1PF01_i3, GEO86500d_Te1PF01_i5; page 86 GEO86500d_Te1PF01_i6, GEO86500d_Te1PF01_i7, GEO86500d_Te1PF01_i8; page 98 GEO86500d_Te1PF01_i1, GEO86500d_Te1PF02_i1; page 99 GEO86500d_Te1PF02_i2, GEO86500d_Te2PF02_Trigonias, GEO86500d_Te2PF02_Teleoceras; page 100 GEO86500d_Te2PF02_Menodus, GEO86500d_Te2PF02_Moropus, GEO86500d_Te2PF02_Oxydactylus; page 101 GEO86500d_Te2PF02_Gomphotherium, GEO86500d_Te2PF02_Perchoerus, GEO86500d_Te2PF02_Archaeotherium; page 102 GEO86500d_Te2PF03_i1, GEO86500d_Te2PF03_i2, GEO86500d_Te2PF02_Homalodotherium; page 103 GEO86500d_Te2PF02_Craumauchenia, GEO86500d_Te2PF03_i4, GEO86500d_Te2PF03_i6; page 105 GEO86500d_HomPF02_Pliopithecus, GEO86500d_Proconsul, GEO86500d_HomPF02_Sivapithecus; pages 116–117 GEO86500d_Qu.PP.01; page 121 GEO86500d_QuPF05_i1; page 122 GEO86500d_QuPF05_i3, GEO86500d_QuPF05_i2; page 123 GEO86500d_QuPF05_i4; page 124 GEO86500d_QuPP01_i1, GEO86500d_QuPF04_i1; page 125 GEO86500d_QuPF04_i2, GEO86500d_QuPF04_i3, GEO86500d_QuPF06_i1; back flap GEO86500d_JuCrPF05_i6, GEO86500d_Te2PF03_i1; back cover (clockwise from top right) images 1–3 GEO86500d_JuCrPF03_i1, GEO86500d_CbPmPF04_i8, GEO86500d_Te2PF02_Menodus; images 5–7 GEO86500d_JuCrPF11_i6, GEO86500d_Te1PF02_i2, GEO86500d_QuPF05_i4

© The Field Museum, artwork by Charles Knight
Page 26 CK49T; page 68 CK39T; pages 118–119 CK21T; pages 126–127 CK30T

© The Field Museum, artwork by Phlesch Bubble Productions
Front cover (counterclockwise from top left) image 3 *Bathyuriscus*; title page *Canadia*; frontispiece (counterclockwise from top right) image 6 *Pikaia*; foreword image 1 *Opabinia*; pages 14–19; back cover (clockwise from top right) image 4 *Wiwaxia*

Bibliography

Along with the curators, scientists, and other staff at The Field Museum, the authors referenced the following materials.

Beard, C. 2004. *The Hunt for the Dawn Monkey: Unearthing the Origins of Monkeys, Apes, and Humans.* Berkeley: University of California Press.

Begun, D. R. 2003. Planet of the apes. Scientific American, August.

Behrensmeyer, A. K., J. D. Damuth, W. A. DiMichele, R. Potts, H-D. Sues, and S. L. Wing (eds.). 1992. *Terrestrial Ecosystems Through Time: Evolutionary Paleoecology of Terrestrial Plants and Animals.* Chicago: The University of Chicago Press.

Boardman, R. S., A. H. Cheetham, and A. J. Rowell. 1987. *Fossil Invertebrates.* Palo Alto: Blackwell Scientific Publications.

Briggs, D. E. G., D. H. Erwin, and F. J. Collier. 1994. *The Fossils of the Burgess Shale.* Washington: Smithsonian Institution Press.

Brusca, R., and G. Brusca. 1990. *Invertebrates.* Sunderland: Sinauer Associates, Inc.

Carroll, R. L. 1988. *Vertebrate Paleontology and Evolution.* New York: W. H. Freeman and Company.

Carroll, R. L., K. A. Bossy, A. C. Milner, S. M. Andrews, and C. F. Wellstead. 1998. Lepospodyli. Handbuch der Palaoherpetologie 1.

Clack, J. A. 2002. *Gaining Ground: The Origin and Evolution of Tetrapods.* Bloomington: Indiana University Press.

Darwin, C. 1964. *On the Origin of Species: A Facsimile of the First Edition.* Cambridge: Harvard University Press.

Everhart, M. J. 2005. *Oceans of Kansas.* Bloomington: Indiana University Press.

Farlow, J. O., and M. K. Brett-Surman (eds.). 1997. *The Complete Dinosaur.* Indiana: Indiana University Press.

Fastovsky, D. E., and D. B. Weishampel. 2005. *The Evolution and Extinction of the Dinosaurs, Second Edition.* Cambridge: Cambridge University Press.

Fortey, R. 2000. *Trilobites: Eyewitness to Evolution.* New York: Vintage Books.

Glut, D. F. 1997. *Dinosaurs: The Encyclopedia.* North Carolina: McFarland & Company, Inc., Publishers.

Gould, S. J. (ed.). 2001. *The Book of Life: An Illustrated History of the Evolution of Life on Earth, Second Edition.* New York: W. W. Norton & Company, Inc.

Grande, L. 1984. Paleontology of the Green River Formation, with a review of the fish fauna. The Geological Survey of Wyoming, Bulletin 63.

Grande, L. 1998. This Land: Fossil Lake. Natural History 107(6):66–69.

Grande, L. 2001. An updated review of the fish faunas from the Green River Formation, the world's most productive freshwater lagerstatten. In *Eocene Biodiversity: Unusual Occurrences and Rarely Sampled Habitats.* Edited by Gregg F. Gunnell. New York: Kluwer Academic/Plenum Publishers.

Grimaldi, D., and M. S. Engel. 2005. *Evolution of the Insects.* New York: Cambridge University Press.

Johanson, D. C., and B. Edgar. 2006. *From Lucy to Language: Revised, Updated, and Expanded.* New York: Simon & Schuster Editions.

Kenrick, P., and P. Davis. 2004. *Fossil Plants.* Smithsonian Books.

Kielan-Jaworowska, Z., R. L. Cifelli, and Z-X. Luo. 2004. *Mammals from the Age of Dinosaurs: Origins, Evolution, and Structure.* New York: Columbia University Press.

King, G. M. 1988. Anomodontia. Handbuch der Palaoherpetologie 17C.

Knoll, A. 2003. *Life on a Young Planet.* Princeton: Princeton University Press.

Lecointre, G., and H. Le Guyader. 2006. *The Tree of Life: A Phylogenetic Classification.* Cambridge: The Belknap Press of Harvard University Press.

Levi-Setti, R.1993. *Trilobites, Second Edition.* Chicago: The University of Chicago Press.

Macdougall, D. 2004. *Frozen Earth: The Once and Future Story of Ice Ages.* Berkeley and Los Angeles: University of California Press.

MacFadden, B. J. 1992. *Fossil Horses: Systematics, Paleobiology, and Evolution of the Family Equidae.* New York: Cambridge University Press.

Multiple authors. 2004. Dinosaurs and other monsters. Scientific American, June.

Maisey, J. G. 2000. *Discovering Fossil Fishes.* Colorado: Westview Press.

Reisz, R. R. 1986. Pelycosauria. Handbuch der Palaoherpetologie 17A.

Rieppel, O. 2000. Sauropterygia I: Placodontia, Pachypleurosauria, Nothosauroidea, Pistosauroidea. Handbuch der Palaoherpetologie 12A.

Romer, A. S. and L. I. Price. 1940. Review of the Pelycosauria. Geological Society of America Special Papers 28.

Savage, D. E., and D. E. Russell. 1983. *Mammalian Paleofaunas of the World.* Reading: Addison-Wesley Publishing Company, Inc.

Selim, J. 2004. Useless body parts. Discover, June.

Shabica, C. W., and A. A. Hay. 1997. *Richardson's Guide to the Fossil Fauna of Mazon Creek.* Chicago: Northeastern Illinois University.

Sigogneau-Russell, D. 1989. Theriodontia I. Handbuch der Palaoherpetologie 17B/I.

Stewart, W. N., and G. W. Rothwell. 1993. *Paleobotany and the Evolution of Plants, Second Edition.* Australia: Cambridge University Press.

Turner, A. 1997. *The Big Cats and Their Fossil Relatives.* New York: Columbia University Press.

Turner, A. 2004. *National Geographic: Prehistoric Mammals.* Washington, D.C.: Firecrest Books Ltd.

Valentine, J. W. 2004. *On the Origin of Phyla.* Chicago: University of Chicago Press.

Weishampel, D. B., P. Dodson, and H. Osmolska (eds.). 2005. *The Dinosauria, Second Edition.* Berkeley: University of California Press.

Wellnhofer, P. 1991. *The Illustrated Encyclopedia of Pterosaurs.* London: Salamander Books Limited.

Willis, K. J., and J. C. McElwain. 2002. *The Evolution of Plants.* New York: Oxford University Press.

Wilson, E. O. 1992. *The Diversity of Life.* New York: W. W. Norton & Company.

Wittry, J. 2006. *The Mazon Creek Fossil Flora.* Downers Grove: Esconi Associates.

Woodburne, M. O., and C. C. Swisher, III. 1995. Land mammal high-resolution geochronology, intercontinental overland dispersals, sea level, climate, and vicariance. Geochronology Time Scales and Global Stratigraphic Correlation, SEPM Special Publication 54:335–364.

Index